SUCCEEDING THROUGH DOUBT, FEAR AND CRISIS

Dear Cecile,

I wish you every good thing you wish for yourself. You are a lovely bright light!

Blessings,
Mary Beth

SUCCEEDING THROUGH DOUBT, FEAR AND CRISIS

Presented by Sandra Yancey

Presented by: Sandra Yancey

Producer: Ruby Yeh

Editorial Director: AJ Harper

Print Management: Book Lab

Cover Design: Keith Speegle

Book Design & Typesetting: Chinook Design, Inc.

ISBN-13: 978-0-9891792-9-4

Printed in the United States of America

Contents

CONTENTS

Introduction

Three days before the annual eWomenNetwork Conference was scheduled to start, I changed my opening keynote. Now, I'm not the type of person who asks for last-minute changes, but after the year I had and the transformation I experienced, I felt compelled to change it.

The speech I planned to give had been set for months. I would come out on stage with flames on the screens behind me, wearing a red dress, to "This Girl Is On Fire" by Alicia Keys. The Tuesday before my Friday keynote, I went into the office, but soon after had this feeling: *I have to get out of here.*

I went home. It was August and very hot, so I got myself a glass of ice water and sat on my patio. Restless, I turned on the radio and heard a song I'd never heard before—"Brave" by Sara Bareilles. "What are these words?" I said. After the song was over, I kept thinking about it and thinking about it, and finally went to my home office to Google the lyrics.

The song discusses having enough courage to tell the truth about who you are. *I've got to be brave enough to tell my story,* I thought. It took me all of five minutes to decide. I called my office and said, "I know you're going to hate me, but I'm going to ask you to support me in something. I have to change everything in the opening."

We often think that nobody has it as bad we do. We often think that other people can't possibly be experiencing what we're experiencing. We often think that no one can overcome the depth of struggle we've had. That's what is so great about this book— it allows you to see that we're all different in exactly the same way. In this book, you'll read stories about people who have had similar—or more devastating—experiences. These authors have had the opportunity to rethink, retool, revitalize and reclaim their power.

If one of these stories helps someone who otherwise thinks they are not going to make it, then this is probably one of the most valuable books on the planet.

We often think that other people
can't possibly be experiencing
what we're experiencing.

The idea for this book came to me when I looked at the recent statistics about women entrepreneurs. When I started eWomenNetwork fourteen years ago, only two percent of all women business owners ever broke one million dollars in annual revenue. Here we are, moving into our fifteenth year, and the needle hasn't moved. The ability to become a successful entrepreneur is so much greater than it was when we started—in 2000 we didn't have social media or YouTube, and Kinko's was just "that copy place." And yet we're still staring at the same statistics, wondering what it will take to see real change.

I believe we've been stuck at two percent because we keep looking outside of ourselves for solutions. It's very important to get the best resources, vendors, consultants, ideas and strategies, but not at the expense of looking at what's happening with us on the inside. What really holds us back is our inner glass ceiling, the unconscious barrier that we create by letting our "stinkin' thinkin'" get the best of us. Our self-critique manifests as doubt and fear, as drama around whatever crises we've been through, and all of this prevents us from stepping into our magnificence.

You have to listen to your heart, because it will always remind you what you're missing.

My intention in starting eWomenNetwork was to create a massive movement of women entrepreneurs supporting other women entrepreneurs around the world. What I didn't know was that it would take much more effort to maintain a global multimillion-dollar enterprise than it took to grow it! It's easy to get there the first time; the hard work is staying there. The business was always hungry, and I was always feeding it.

As business leaders, we're trained and encouraged to think logically in order to succeed. The funny thing is, while logic may lead you to success, your heart will lead you to fulfillment, and success and fulfillment are two different results. I didn't really understand this when I started eWomenNetwork.

You have to listen to your heart, because it will always remind you what you're missing. Your heart has its own language, and sometimes you have to quiet your mind so you can hear it. For several years, I didn't pay attention to what my heart was telling me. I kept thinking strategically and, in the process of making all of those moves, I lost my sense of personal fulfillment. I started to realize that something wasn't resonating with me when I noticed symptoms: I was exhausted; I started gaining five or six pounds a year, which, after, five years, really adds up; the outside noise was often too much for me; and I craved solitude.

At the same time, I was dealing with massive change in our family. My mother's health had deteriorated, and we had to move her from her home in Ohio so she could be close to us in Dallas. As her executor, there was a lot for me to handle. My son was getting ready to graduate high school and move on to college, a phase of my mothering coming to an end.

My daughter was getting married, and what was a beautiful and exciting time for both of us, was also at times sad for me. My role as her mother was changing, and there was a need for closure, for mourning. I kept thinking, *Is she ready? Did I do everything I was supposed to do? Did I teach her all of the lessons I wanted her to*

If your dreams don't scare you, you're not thinking big enough.

---

have in order to become an independent woman, a strong woman, a great wife? Handling all of this in the midst of a thirty-city tour was beyond difficult. Then, our family dog died unexpectedly.

It was in the quiet moments, at the end of the day, that I got real with myself. I'm very good at justifying my behavior when I think it will serve me, but when I looked in the mirror, I could no longer deny it. I said, "Okay, Sandra, what is going on with you?" I didn't like the way I looked. I didn't like the way I felt. I realized I was in a personal crisis, and it was a very lonely place. Staring into my own eyes, I said, "How can you expect magnificence to come into your life if you don't have the energy to manage it?"

So often, when you have a lot of demands on you, you give up the very things that feed your *soul*. I started going back to the things that were true for me, things that I had given up in order to feed my business. I started meditating again. I hired a trainer to teach me how to exercise using just my own body, so I could work out on the road. I started focusing on the aspects of business I love and do best, rather than every detail and request.

It was a time of profound transformation—which, let me tell you, was scary for me, and for the people who loved me. I came back to myself, but that required everyone around me to adjust. Fear is a funny thing. When I stand before an audience and ask, "What does the acronym FEAR stand for?" a chorus of people will recite the same answer, in unison: "false evidence appearing real."

With that definition, FEAR is a scary acronym because it suggests that our imagination has gone awry, that our fears are dangerous hallucinations that are to be avoided at all costs. I say, why ignore it? Why pretend fear isn't real? In my experience, fear is simply a sign that we are on the edge of something new.

I believe in my heart that we need to have a better relationship with fear. What would happen if, rather than push away our feelings of anxiety and trepidation, we embraced them? The truth is, comfort is achievement's number one enemy. When we feel afraid it means we are leaving our comfort zone—and that is a step toward greatness.

If your dreams don't scare you, you're not thinking big enough. For me, FEAR is now an acronym for "feel everything and rise." Feel nervous, feel worried, feel doubtful, feel scared, and then

---

I spoke from my heart—about losing myself and finding my purpose again.

---

move on. Massive success is on the other side of fear, and the only way to *get* to the other side is embrace it, take it in, feel all of it, and move forward strong in the certainty that you are on the verge of something amazing.

After changing my speech, my song, my dress and my set design, I walked out onto the stage at the eWomenNetwork Conference; I faced my fear and walked through it, just as I had done when I decided to make a change and rise out of my personal crisis. I spoke from my heart about losing myself and finding my purpose again. About how, by listening to that little voice inside me, and valuing my *no* as much as my *yes*, I regained a sense of fulfillment. And I shared the most important lesson I learned in the past two years: "No one is responsible for rescuing me but me. How could I ask somebody to do for me what I was least willing to do for myself?"

I feel more centered, more vibrant, more connected and more purposeful than I have felt in a long time. And I know my co-authors are also living fulfilled lives, successfully building businesses and sharing their stories with the world. *With you*. I'm impressed by their willingness to write about some of their most vulnerable moments in order to serve others, to inspire others, to give tips and ideas and strategies to help others navigate the fog of doubt, fear and crisis. This book is a testament to their strength... and your possibilities.

No matter the reason you picked up this book, know that, in these pages you will find the inspiration for a new song, the wisdom with which to write a new speech, and the courage to walk out onto your very own stage and face your audience while standing firmly in your truth.

Hyrum W. Smith

Misery Is Optional

Three weeks after 9/11, the office of then-Mayor Rudy Giuliani called me from New York. I had met Rudy in 1987 when we were honored together at a dinner in Washington, D.C. A member of his staff asked if my partner Steven Covey and I would come to New York to do a workshop for the families affected by the tragedy. They said, "The Midtown Sheraton has donated their ballroom and hotel rooms. We can't pay you. We can't even pay your airfare."

Without hesitation I said, "We'll come. When do you need us?"

On October 18th, 2001, Steven and I flew to New York. I'd flown into New York hundreds of times. In fact, I was at Bayside High School before they built the World Trade Center towers; I actually watched the towers being built in the early 60s. This time, though, flying over the East River was a very different experience. The World Trade Center was gone. We flew in late at night and from our window we could see lights and smoke. It was a surreal experience.

The mayor had arranged a tour of Ground Zero for Steve and myself. The next morning at five a.m., a police van picked us up and took us to the site. After getting through four police checkpoints, I stood on fifteen feet of compacted debris in front of the largest hole I'd ever seen.

Our police escort pointed toward the Merrill Lynch building and said, "I was here that day. I was standing right there and all of a sudden I heard this big boom. I looked up and all this stuff started flying out of the towers. It looked like paper at first and then it started hitting the ground, and I realized they were fifty foot I-beams. I watched thirty-four people jump from the tower. Four of them were holding hands. I watched eight firefighters lose their lives because people fell on them."

Oh my gosh, I thought, overcome with the enormity of it all.

Then he asked, "How many computers do you think were in the World Trade Center?"

"Well," I said, "fifty thousand people worked in the towers. I bet there were a lot of computers." When the officer told me they hadn't found one computer, I said, "You're kidding. How come?"

"Three thousand degree fire, man. And it's still burning."

As he told more of his story, a crane pulled an I-beam out of the rubble. It was dripping molten steel out of one end. The

---

*I stood on fifteen feet of compacted debris
in front of the largest hole I'd ever seen.*

---

officer finished his story and said, "When the second tower came down, I thought I was dead. I got under a truck and somehow survived."

That's how the day started.

After returning to our room to shower off the soot, Steven and I went to lead the workshop. In a ballroom designed for a capacity of eighteen hundred, twenty-three hundred people were jammed into every space available. The event began with two police officers and two firefighters in dress uniforms walking in with the American flag, and that about wiped me out. Then, the Harlem Girls Choir blew the roof off singing three patriotic songs. I've never heard more magnificent music.

By then, I was bawling like a baby. I was grateful Steven was up first. When it was my turn to speak, I made my way to the front of the room, stepping over people sitting on the floor. Before I could open my mouth, a firefighter about halfway back stood up and said, "Mr. Smith, are you going to tell us how we're going to get out of bed in the morning, when we just don't give a crap anymore?"

And that is how one of the toughest and most rewarding speaking experiences I've ever had began.

I looked out at the expectant, shocked, grief-stricken faces of

Pain is inevitable; misery is optional.

the audience, and then turned to the firefighter and said, "If you remember one thing I say today, let it be these words: Pain is inevitable; misery is optional."

"The fact is, bad things happen to good people. Wars happen. People lose their 401ks. Tsunamis wipe out villages in Thailand. Nuclear plants crash. A lot of bad stuff happens. We're not going to get through this mortal experience without some pain. How we choose to deal with that pain ultimately is the measure of who we are."

Then I said, "When you compare what happened here on 9/11 to what has happened on this planet in the last one hundred and fifty years, it doesn't even come up on the scope of ugliness in comparison. Does it?"

It was so quiet in that massive room you could hear a pin drop.

"Let's go back to June 5, 1944," I continued. "Eisenhower is in a bunker in England and says to his generals, 'Gentleman, we've got to throw more kids at that beach in Normandy tomorrow than the Germans have bullets in their bunkers.' The next day they threw two hundred thousand kids at that beach. And do you know what happened? The Germans ran out of bullets in their bunkers. Eisenhower had estimated within four hundred how many young men he'd lose. How often do we remember that?"

I went on to remind the audience of other tragic and monumental losses. Nearly half a million kids lost in WWII, more than six hundred thousand lost in the Civil War—we lost fifty thousand soldiers in three days at Gettysburg. Korea. Vietnam. The list goes on.

Then I said, "Let me tell you why this means so much to me. On May 18, 1995, my two daughters were driving home from Salt Lake City. My daughter Sharwan, twenty-five and three weeks away from her wedding, and Stacie, twenty-seven,

---

For the first time in my life, I experienced
very deep unbelievable pain.

---

who had her two-year-old daughter with her in the car, had an accident. They rolled the car. Sharwan was killed instantly and my granddaughter was thrown from the car and killed instantly. Somehow, Stacie survived."

"For the first time in my life, I experienced very deep unbelievable pain. I had to call Stacie's husband and say, 'Your wife is in the hospital in critical condition and your daughter is dead.' I had to call Sharwan's fiancé and tell him she was dead."

I looked out into the room at thousands of pairs of eyes fixed on me, no doubt remembering the heart-wrenching phone calls they'd had to make after 9/11. Then I said, "Early in the morning before the funeral of my daughter and granddaughter, I sat in my office trying to come up with something to say. How do you speak at your own daughter's funeral? You always expect to outlive your kids.

"There's a painting in my office that's been there forever. My forebears were all pioneers. They came out west back in 1847 by wagon train. It was a pretty tough way to travel. It took three months to go one thousand miles. The painting depicts a winter scene, a couple standing over a grave of a family member they've just buried. As I sat there in my office, staring at the painting, I saw something I'd never noticed before. In the background were other wagons and people sitting on the wagons, holding the reins of their horses. They were waiting for this couple to finish burying their loved one. That's when I realized what the pioneers knew, and what we have to learn: We have to move on, or we will not survive."

Even as tears streamed down their faces, I could see recognition in the faces of the audience. At that moment, they knew I understood their pain. I said, "There are times when I still get mad as hell about losing my daughter and granddaughter,

---

Everyone on the planet has
to deal with some pain.

---

but we have to move on. It changed me; it forever changed my outlook on life and I will never forget. But if I had decided to be miserable, it would have ruined many other lives, my own included."

Speaking in New York that day was an unbelievable experience. Afterwards, the audience broke up into smaller groups and I rotated between them. People were weeping. It was a cathartic day. People hugged me and said, "We can deal with this." I knew then that many of them had already made the crucial choice: They would not let the tragedy of 9/11 claim another life; they would not choose misery.

Everyone on the planet has to deal with some pain. It's difficult to start and build a business. Three of us started a business in my basement that grew to four thousand people with offices in seventeen countries. We grew to be a billion-dollar corporation, but it started with just three people who were willing to get beat up by the difficulties that come when you start a business.

Three basic emotions motivate everything you do and they are hierarchal in nature. The lowest emotion is fear. Some of us go to work out of fear. "If I don't work, I won't get paid and I'll starve." Fear is a great motivator.

A little higher on the list is a sense of duty. If duty motivates you, you might say, "I go to work because I've been raised with the ethic that says 'give a full day's effort for a full day's pay.'" Or you might choose to do something because you're under contract to do so, or because it's the law.

The third and highest emotion that motivates activity is love.

Fear is "I have to." Duty is "I ought to." Love is "I want to."

We are here on this planet to journey from fear to love. How much energy surrounds a project when you do it out of fear or obligation? Hardly any. How much energy will you have if you are

---

Fear is "I have to." Duty is "I ought to." Love is "I want to."

---

doing it because you want to, because you love it? Unbelievable energy. And so what happens when you choose to not to be miserable? You immediately take a step toward that higher level, toward love.

If you choose misery, you're done. You're toast. Your mind shuts down and you stop thinking about the things you ought to think about to build and strengthen your relationships, your body, your mind and your business. And if you chose misery, everybody around you is also miserable. The endgame for misery is hopelessness.

Misery is a choice. No one is running your life but you. Make the decision to function out of love, not fear. When you choose love, that's when miracles happen.

Hyrum W. Smith is a distinguished author, speaker, and businessman. Co-founder and former CEO of Franklin Covey, Co., for three decades he has been empowering people to effectively govern their personal and professional lives. Hyrum combines wit and enthusiasm with a gift for communicating compelling principles that incite lasting personal change. The author of several nationally-acclaimed books, including The 10 Natural Laws of Successful Time and Life Management, What Matters Most *and* The Modern Gladiator, *his most recent work is* The Power of Perception: 6 Rules of Behavior Change. *He is currently writing a book with Spencer Johnson and Ken Blanchard,* What's on Your Belief Window? *Connect with Hyrum at www.HyrumWSmith.com.*

Adrian Halperin

The Yellow Feather

On a dark Friday night of Labor Day weekend, 1963, my father prepared to leave everything he knew behind. He loaded up the station wagon, coordinated with a friend to help him with the three-day drive from Florida to Canada and said his goodbyes to his mother.

I was eight years old when my father fled the United States with two of my siblings and me to avoid complying with a court order granting custody of us to my mother, his ex-wife. He walked out on his engineering job at Cape Canaveral and a lifetime pension from the Army; after serving nineteen years and eleven months, he was just one month shy of retirement.

He had cared for us for years. He saw us every day and raised us according to his values. He just couldn't live with being only a "weekend dad."

My first memory is a happy one. I was about three or four years old. I remember Dad smoking a cigar on the screened-in porch of the little rambler home we lived in on Lancelot Lane in Winston-Salem, North Carolina. Mom was standing in the doorway to the house, laughing and smiling. I'm not sure why this memory stands out, but it may have something to do with what happened next.

My parents split up, and my father took my older sister, younger brother and me to Florida to live with his parents. In 1962, four years later, a woman I didn't recognize showed up at our back door with a baby on her hip. In a stern voice, Dad said, "Go play outside," and invited her in.

That woman was my mother, who had moved to Florida with the hope of reconciling with my father. Evidently they had seen each other several times over the years, and the baby, my little sister, was the result of their visits. My father told me that because he didn't want anything to do with my mother, she took him to court. When the Florida court overruled the North Carolina court, granting custody to my mother, we began visiting her home on weekends. When school was about to start, the court ruled that we must live with our mother full-time, which would mean seeing our father only on weekends.

My father was so angry—angry with my mother and angry at the court system that routinely granted custody to mothers.

It would just be Dad and us.

He told me our mother didn't want us when we were in North Carolina and now had changed her mind. When he told me his plan to run away with us, he said, "It's not going to be easy. We won't have a lot of money at first and we're going to have to keep it a secret."

I quickly realized that we would no longer have the security and safety of living with our father and grandmother. It would just be Dad and us. On the other hand, if we stayed, I would have to adjust to living with a mother I was only beginning to get acclimated to, going to a new school and getting to know my maternal grandmother, who always seemed stern and strict.

Somehow, the prospect of staying in Florida to start a new life with my mom seemed like a bigger risk than leaving with my dad—who had been my primary caregiver for four years—to have an adventure. At eight years old, I didn't know he was breaking the law. What I knew for sure was, I loved my dad. My mom, I barely knew.

My father's warning about the road ahead hanging in the air, and so much at stake, I looked at him and said, "Dad, you can take the forty dollars out of my savings account if you need to. You can use that."

I had earned that money by making little potholders and painting seashells, selling them for nickels and pennies. Yet despite all of that hard work, I didn't hesitate to offer the money to him. He was my dad, and I would have followed him anywhere.

My dad was the only parent I knew, and I didn't want to be responsible for him going to jail.

A few days before Labor Day weekend, we went to visit our mother knowing it would be the last time. Dad had instructed us to take anything we could fit into the one Army footlocker he planned to take. All I knew about Canada was that it could get very cold, so I hid my ivory-colored sweater in a three-ring binder, thinking Mom would let me take the binder for school and wouldn't notice the sweater stuffed inside. But she did.

When I was getting into her black Ford, she said, "Why are you taking your sweater?"

"Oh, I… I just wanted to have it in case we're going to the beach," I explained, and then ran back into the house and left the sweater on the kitchen table. Mom drove us over to Dad's, we said goodbye as if it were any other day, and she drove away. There were no poignant goodbyes, no special words. That was it.

Dad and his friend shared the driving, pushing hard until we reached Washington, D.C. There, we put his friend on a plane to go back to Florida. We would make the rest of the trip on our own. Dad hadn't coached us on what to say, but it had been ingrained in us early on not to chime in or interrupt adults. So when the uniformed man at the border leaned in the window to ask where were going and how long we planned to stay in Canada, we didn't make a peep.

Over the next five years, we lived in three different towns in Canada. In the first apartment, we were four people crowded into two bedrooms, all of us sleeping on bunk beds. I wasn't aware of how Dad operated under his new identity, but we kept ours. I remember he said once, "If someone shows up at the door and tells you he's an insurance agent and he's looking for me, don't tell him anything. He could be a police officer pretending. If they find us, I could go to jail." I was so afraid to answer the door. My dad was the only parent I knew, and I didn't want to be responsible for him going to jail.

He was never caught, and we remained with our father, whom I supported without question. My sister, who was older and had more memories of our mother, did not. She believed that her

*I started to follow a path that would
lead me to do things I wanted to do.*

childhood had been taken from her and questioned his choices.

When I was a sophomore in college living in New York, she decided to track down our mother. I don't know how she knew that Mom had married a man with five children and was living in the Orlando area. Through one of those children, she was able to get Mom's number. When she told me she'd found Mom, I said, "I'm not ready. Please don't give her my contact info."

The next thing I knew, I got a phone call. "Adrian, this is your mother." I was shocked. I had no idea how to respond. It was an odd conversation—how could it not be, after everything?

Soon after, she and her husband flew us down to Florida for a visit. As I walked through the airport, I looked at each of the women who seemed to be about her age and thought, *Are you my mom? Are you my mom?*

The only picture we had of my mother was of the three of us with her on our front porch back in North Carolina, standing there in our bathing suits. She had dark brown hair and big glasses, the kind Mary Tyler Moore wore on the *Dick Van Dyke Show*. Growing up, I always thought Mom looked like Mary Tyler Moore and when I watched the *Dick Van Dyke Show*, I would think, *That's what life would be like if we were all together.* But that was just a fantasy. The reality was, I didn't know my mother at all.

**You can choose who you are today, and
who you will become tomorrow.**

Over the next eight years, Mom and I stayed in touch. Though we never had the type of mother-daughter relationship many women have, it was very rewarding getting to know about her life. When I got married, her husband offered to pay for my wedding; I refused his offer. My own father couldn't afford it.

Dad's influence stayed with me throughout my life. I had the opportunity to represent my high school in a national beauty pageant, but I declined, fearing discovery. Rather than pursue an art career, I followed his advice and chose a practical option, something safe. I worked hard to be a good breadwinner, to make him, and others proud of me. And I continued to defend him when my sister grumbled about our childhood. I always said, "Look how much he gave up to raise us—he must really love us."

Then, in 1995, everything changed. My husband called and said, "Your dad died suddenly. It was a heart attack."

After we buried him, a flood of emotions consumed me. I had an emotional breakdown. The man who raised me, whom I had loved so dearly, whom I had defended for his actions, was gone. *I don't have to hide anymore.* I no longer have to protect him.

I remembered a recurring dream I'd had most of my life. In the dream, I'm walking through the woods with my older sister, my brother and Dad. We're all wearing backpacks, finding our way along a creek. Every time I look down at the water, I see a yellow feather floating by. I'd always wondered what the yellow feather meant, and then it became clear: Deep down, I wondered if his actions were, in part, cowardly. Rather than fight the system, he ran. It was a selfish move.

I had viewed my father as a selfless man who sacrificed his job, his pension and his home to "save us" from our mother's influence. With the help of a therapist, after his death I realized that Dad taking us from Mom was a violent act. He couldn't get what he wanted through the court system and, by taking us from her physically, he robbed us of a relationship with our mother and sister.

Soon, I stopped thinking I had to make excuses for my father's choices, and this inspired me to examine *my own* choices. I started to follow a path that would lead me to do things I wanted to do, not just things to please or protect my father. I hadn't been happy in my marriage, and my lucrative job was beyond stressful. I wasn't putting my two children to bed at night, and most days I was a nervous wreck. It was time to find the courage to change. I would not become that yellow feather in the water.

Leaving my job was scary. Leaving my marriage was even more difficult, but we were committed to making it as easy on the children as possible. Because of my experience growing up, I wanted to make sure they had time with both parents. It took a lot of courage for me to stay in the town my ex-husband lived in, because I faced a lot of judgment from the community. But I stuck it out, so that I could co-parent and give my children the stable childhood I had not had.

I returned to my first love: interior design. Without any income, I leapt into the unknown. Not long after, I bought my own interior design franchise.

Eventually, by facing my feelings and honoring my own opinions and desires, I was able to make peace with my father's choices. Now I know that, although his actions were cowardly, he was doing the best he could with the skills he had at the time.

Before she passed away, Mom told us that when she remarried, her husband, a Florida state trooper and owner of a bail bond company at the time, offered to help her find us. She said, "It was then that I realized you were with your father; it wasn't as if you'd been taken by a stranger. I knew he cared for you and I didn't want to disrupt your lives. So I told him 'no thank you.'"

Mom loved us; she let us be. I was never more certain of how deeply she loved me until, after her death, I received a package from my younger sister. My stepfather had passed away, and in order to have equity among all of the kids, everything was appraised. If we wanted something, we bought it from the estate. I purchased a silver punch bowl with punch glasses.

My sister, who had been left with Mom, said, "I'm sending something I think Mom would want you to have; It's the right time."

When I opened the box, I was speechless. There inside of the punch bowl was my ivory sweater, the one I had tried to take with me the day we left for Canada. I remembered that my grandmother had stitched my name into the label, and there it was: *Adrian*. Fifty years later, I held the sweater in my hands. Mom had kept it with her all those years.

You can't choose your birthplace or your parents. However, in spite of hearing, "Your mother didn't want you," I know God doesn't make junk. Whatever your circumstances, you can overcome them. You can find your voice. You can honor your past, forgive those who loved you the best they could and carve out a new path. You can choose who you are today, and who you will become tomorrow.

Adrian Halperin, Allied ASID, is an internationally recognized healthy home interior designer. Known as the "House Doctor," she is passionate about providing her clients with healthy, safe and beautiful furnishings that fit their lifestyle without making them sick. Decorating since 1999, Adrian has served hundreds of clients in New York and other East Coast cities, Chicago, North Carolina and now Central Florida. In addition to decorating individual and family homes, she works with condo associations and businesses such as The Library of the Smithsonian National Institute, Fitness Together and Capitol Bank.

After fifteen years of designing beautiful spaces and teaching design principles to decorators and clients, Adrian saw a distinct need in the interior furnishings marketplace. A client came to her seeking advice on furnishings for her home that would not make her sick. Recently diagnosed with Lyme disease, she needed a sofa that would not cause her to go into respiratory distress. Helping this client was an awakening for Adrian. As she searched to find furnishings to help her suffering friend, she saw the very serious need for healthy home furnishings.

Featured in numerous publications, including Decorating Solutions *magazine,* The Complete Guide to Decorating, *and* Decorating… The Professional Touch, *Adrian was part of the National Symphony Orchestra's Decorator Showhouse and won first place for the International Dream Room contest (Model Show House category). Adrian is currently writing a book about her family. Connect with Adrian at www.HouseDrx.com.*

Cass Mullane

The Cool Stuff Jar

I t started with a sticky note.

One day, about twenty-five years ago, one of my bosses gave me a really nice memo. On top of the memo he placed a yellow sticky note that said, "Nice job, Cass." I wanted a reminder of it, so I took the sticky note off the memo and stuck it in a little bowl in my desk drawer, way in the back. It wasn't my intention to fill up the bowl, but in the weeks and months that followed, I started jotting down onto slips of paper the good things that happened and dropping the slips into the bowl.

About a year later, I moved offices. When I was clearing out my desk I noticed the bowl overflowing with tiny little notes, so I dumped the notes into an envelope and took it home. That night, I read every single note. What had been just a simple reminder of a job well done had become a collection of all of my accomplishments at work that year, big and small.

I looked at the brightly colored mound of good and awesome things I'd learned, attempted and pulled off that year and realized, "I should use this for my annual review."

At the time, I was a shy, quiet introvert working in a corporate environment. I was really good at my job, responsible for some very important projects and programs, but I rarely stood up for myself or fought to be recognized. Until I saved the "nice job" sticky note, I hadn't kept track of my good work or the results I generated for the company.

Now, I had dozens of reference points for my review, evidence that I was valuable. As I re-filled the bowl with all of the new good things I'd done at work, my confidence grew. Every time I looked at the stack of messages, surrounded by colorful lines and doodles, I felt strong and happy. Those positive feelings stayed with me all day.

Slowly, my mindset shifted, and I began to see myself in a different light. *So what if I'm shy? I'm also very creative, innovative and competent.* Keeping track of all of my awesomeness at work gave me the courage to actually *say*, "Hey, I am creative. I am innovative. I am competent," and start going after projects I wouldn't have gone after before. When you start telling people your value, you have to back it up. I followed through on promises

-----

Now, I had dozens of reference points for my review, evidence that I was valuable.

-----

and earned respect from my peers and my superiors for doing great work, and with that came promotions and greater responsibility. Eventually, I attracted the right people to my team, and together we got amazing things done. Everyone was in top performance mode.

Through it all, I kept track of all of the good stuff—whether it was finishing a project ahead of schedule or solving a tough problem or coming up with a new idea or strategy. By doing that simple, concrete action which reinforced my value, I was able to break through the glass ceiling. It took a lot of work to get there, but I did it. I did it by discovering and acknowledging the innate power within me that I was only able to see, finally, because I had tangible evidence.

Slowly, note by note, index card by index card, I stepped into my own greatness. That little bowl eventually became a jar. I call it my Cool Stuff Jar.

After the first few years, I started adding notes about all of the cool stuff that I experienced, little things that make life rich and resplendent. I'm on my third jar now. (I've broken the other two!)

Slowly, note by note, index card by index card, I stepped into my own greatness.

It's an old-style glass cookie jar, small and squatty, with a wide rim. I fill it with cut-up colored file cards and art papers that have cool things written on them, everything from "Kicked off a new Rockin' 2014! Webinar with attendees from US, Canada, Scotland, England, Australia and Argentina," to, "The sky is gorgeous this afternoon."

My Cool Stuff Jar is a concrete, visual reminder that, even when something lousy is going on, there's a lot of good in my life. It keeps me grounded and positive and changes my outlook in a powerful way. I'm always on the lookout for something new to put in my jar, which means I'm in a near constant state of appreciation and gratitude. If something "jar worthy" happens, I do a little happy dance and drop a card into the jar.

In 2004, after spending so many years working with really strong left-brainers and squelching my own creativity, I realized I could actually use my creativity to benefit myself and others, so I decided to start my own business. I moved back to Colorado and now enjoy coaching business owners and corporate teams. I specialize in helping right-brainers and creative people build solid business skills, often in a fun, visual manner.

In 2013, Jennifer Lee, the author of *The Right-Brain Business Plan: A Creative, Visual Map for Success,* interviewed me in her Right-Brainers in Business Video Summit Spotlight. I showed her some of my artwork, and my business self-portrait, which I created in textiles.

When we neared the end of the interview, Jennifer said, "Do you have anything else to share?" My Cool Stuff Jar was sitting on my desk, so I picked it up, showed it on camera and talked about it—why I do it, how it works, why it's awesome. The interview was live, so I wasn't able to look at the chat room comments until after we wrapped. What I saw really surprised me. Apparently, when I started talking about my jar, the chat room went crazy with comments and questions. To me, it was just my jar. I thought, *Doesn't everyone have something like this?* It was then that I realized I had created something powerful that could benefit other people.

Not long after the interview, I was nominated for an ATHENA Award for leadership. Getting nominated is a huge deal, and I wasn't expecting it. At the event, when they announced my

---

***I had created something powerful
that could benefit other people.***

---

name, I was able to hear applause and woo hoos in support of my nomination not just at my table, but scattered throughout the ballroom of six hundred people. It blew me away. I didn't think I knew that many people, professionally and personally, and I had no idea I had made such an impact on their lives.

Holy moly, I have this power. What am I going to do with it? Suddenly, the feeling of responsibility I carried with me— responsibility to my friends, my colleagues, my clients, and my community—became exponentially bigger. I realized I could have a much larger impact on the world. I just had no clue how!

The final push that moved me into action came from Sally Hogshead's "How To Fascinate" assessment, which measures, not how I see the world, but how the world sees me. Turns out, the world sees me as "The Rockstar" and celebrates my innovation and passion. It took some getting used to, the thought that I, the behind-the-scenes supportive introvert, could be a Rockstar. But my close friends said, "Of course you're the Rockstar, everyone knows that."

Now, that made me do some internal assessing... and, yes, I am bold, artistic and unorthodox as the assessment suggests. Once I wrapped my head around that, I began to see that I really needed to step up and own my "Rockstar-ness."

That combination of the surprising chat comments about my Cool Stuff Jar, the experience of being nominated for an ATHENA Award and discovering that people view me as "The Rockstar" radically shifted my mindset toward what I wanted to do, how I wanted to play bigger in life and work. My little jar—who'd have thought I could achieve so much with simple cards and notes? But it's more than that, isn't it?

The Cool Stuff Jar is tangible proof that there is a lot of cool stuff in your life. Even though we all experience doubt and fear and crisis, there will always be good stuff at the end. Don't believe me? Well, you wake up every day, right? That's a good thing. The Cool Stuff Jar enables you to have faith in your ability to get through all of it—to overcome doubt, to push past fear, to survive crisis and come out a wiser, stronger, more compassionate person. When you have your own jar, you invariably end up focusing less energy on the lousy stuff and more energy on the good stuff. It just happens.

As you watch your jar fill up, you build up your confidence. You start to recognize how amazing you really are, not in some fluffy way, but in a meaty, foundational way. You re-frame your thinking about yourself and your environment and shift your focus toward positive changes. You start to believe that you've got the goods, that you can weather storms, take risks and meet challenges. You can dream big. You can become who you have always wanted to be, who you were meant to be, and show up in the world strong, with an authentic presence and purpose.

By using the Cool Stuff Jar, over time you replace your expectations of failure with expectations of success.

The biggest barrier to success is disbelief—in your worth, in your talents and abilities, in your experiences and skill set. It's important to shift from assuming you're going to fail to assuming that you'll succeed. Some people say they believe they will succeed, but they don't really mean it. We say we'll "fake it 'til we make it," but that only gets you so far.

The magic of the Cool Stuff Jar is that it is tangible. Simply putting a note in the jar is doing something, not faking anything, not wishing, not hoping for change. It's a concrete action. It takes time and persistence, dropping your notes and cards into your own jar, day in and day out, but you *will* experience a shift in mindset. You will reframe your thinking. You'll see those notes piling up and you'll think, "Hmmm, I'm not a failure. I can do better. My dreams *are* doable."

You can do it, but you have to choose it. When your mind monkeys come barreling in, chattering away in that unproductive, negative way, toss them a banana and give yourself space to fill your mind with something better. Then, when you successfully replace stinkin' thinkin' with something better, write it down as a win, do a little happy dance and put it in your jar!

Since 2008, I've created handmade cards to give to clients, colleagues, friends and myself. I made them from hang tags that I inked, painted, printed and tied with fibers. They are Permission Slips that grant permission to do things such as: "Break the Rules," or "Own Your Money," or "Pick Your Perfect Clients" or "Know You Are Enough."

The permission slip I have on my wall right now is: "You are Hereby Granted Permission to Use the Good Stuff." This slip encourages me to tap into what's so good about me and brings it to the forefront as often as possible. And where can I find the good stuff about me? In my Cool Stuff Jar! In this way, the notes are not just reminders of all that I was; they are a promise, a call to action, of who I will become.

So now, it's your turn. It's time to make—and use—your own Cool Stuff Jar. Any jar, box or journal will do. Decorate it however you like—mine has strands of blue and green turquoise beads tied around the rim, and "Cool Stuff Jar" written in funky letters on the side. Next, get a pile of white or colored index cards or leftover art paper and a pack of pens and highlighters. Christen your jar with the first note: "I've got a Cool Stuff Jar!" Then, date it and start filling up your jar.

By using the Cool Stuff Jar, over time you replace your expectations of failure with expectations of success.

After you've filled your jar about halfway, I'd love to hear from you. Visit my website and tell me your story. I want to hear your experience and, perhaps, with your permission, share it with the world. Together, we can make an even *bigger* impact.

I have expectations of success. This holds true both for me and for my clients. I give permission to assume that we are capable of doing what it is that we need to do in order to succeed. We are smart enough, we are strong enough, we are brave enough, we are good enough. We fill the Cool Stuff Jar with these realizations over and over, and they lift us up to a new higher "normal."

Make brave choices, every day. Choose to look at life joyfully, even in the face of doubt, fear or crisis. Replace your expectations of failure with expectations of success. Own the things you do well, and then go do those things!

It starts with one note…

Cass Mullane is an author, speaker, artist and coach, and founder of Prosper Creatively, LLC, a business and personal coaching practice specializing in solid business skills for right-brainers and creatives. Drawing on her own right brain, creative nature and aptitude, Cass developed a whole brain approach that utilizes the left brain skills she acquired in her twenty-plus year career working with law firms and major defense contractors in Washington, D.C., and the right brain skills she's honed as an artist. A highly valued coach, her calm, comfortable approach consistently yields positive results for clients.

Cass holds an MBA and a master's degree in information management. She is active in the Colorado Springs community, serving as a board member on the Southern Colorado Women's Chamber of Commerce, a mentor with Women2Women Mentoring and as the "Artist Wrangler" for the Butterflies & Friends project. She was a 2013 Athena Award Nominee.

In addition to business and personal coaching, Cass regularly speaks, holds workshops and offers online classes. Please visit www. ProsperCreatively.com for details. Cass is also a contemporary textile and mixed media artist with a studio in downtown Colorado Springs at Cottonwood Center for the Arts. She derives great joy in engaging both sides of her brain to maintain a pleasant life balance. You can see her art at www.ProsperCreatively.com.

Carolyn Campora

Warrior on the Hero's Journey

The main thing I remember from college is: Symbolic Logic teaches us there is no true conclusion from a false premise. If you are off center, ungrounded, and then try to take a step or make a decision, you won't get where you want to go.

No amount of wisdom, or instruction or revelation passed down from gurus on high will take you where you want to go if you are not listening from a secure place of strength. Whether they are adversaries or leaders, you cannot see your guides clearly unless you are standing firmly in your life, in the present moment, in your truth. In other words, you can't get there from here.

Begin with the simple precept of honoring where you stand, and then take a step. Every step you take moves you ahead.

My forty-year journey with martial arts began after an incident in a cave on the outskirts of Luxemburg. I had met another girl, both of us just out of college. We were exploring the cave when we encountered a few local boys. My heart started racing when they blocked the entrance with their bodies, trapping us in the cave.

Just before I left for Europe, I had played around with a friend who was a martial artist, roughhousing for the first time since I was a girl playing with my two older brothers. My body remembered. In the cave, I pushed the biggest boy, who was braced in the doorway, and he didn't budge. When I pulled him toward me, I got him off balance and slipped out. Then I went right back in and got the other girl.

I have a natural "protect" instinct. If I'd been born a man and very big, I could have been an NFL offensive lineman! However, I'm a smallish woman. So when I returned from my four-month trip through thirteen countries, I figured if I had some real self-defense skills, I could feel safe traveling to more exotic places.

At the time, I was involved with a small group of Catholics gathered around an esoteric religious order, The Little Brothers of the Gospel, devoted to living the life of Jesus in modern times. One drove a truck for a dry cleaner, one made pizzas, one was a janitor. The brothers lived and said Mass in an East Village railroad flat. When I asked for a recommendation for a self-defense class, a fellow in the group said he had looked into a school recommended by another member, who knew the karate master from her Zen meditation group. My friend was moving, so he couldn't go there, but he warmly recommended it to me. I had no idea martial arts would become my life!

*Begin with the simple precept of
honoring where you stand.*

The school allowed visitors one day a week. I watched a class and was transfixed. Lines of men in white outfits with various color belts were punching and kicking and performing ballet-like forms. Then they sparred with each other, using all these moves in simulated combat. Their intensity, power and beauty were mesmerizing.

When I asked to join, the Korean master informed me that they were in their intensive training mode and were accepting no new students until that was complete. I came back and watched the next week, then joined as soon as I was allowed, July 2, 1973.

I was an artist and loved beauty. So I watched a lot while others practiced. That's how it came to pass that I walked in one day to see the eleven people who began with me wearing green belts. They had been promoted at an event I was not told about, since I was not ready to advance. Yes, Virginia, karate is not a spectator sport!

After this eye-opener, my practice began in earnest. It was hard work, but it was made easier by the direct relationship of effort to result. When I was taught a new move, in my next class I was allowed to learn the next new move if and only if I had mastered the last move. If not, I was re-taught that last move. I could rely on this. It did not depend on whether or not the teacher liked

---

You've mastered a step when you can do it properly when you are at your worst.

---

me, who else was doing the move or how well they did, it only depended on me and my focused effort. No politics, no attitudes, no variation. *What a relief!* I thought. *I can do this.* And I did.

Luciano Pavarotti, legendary for his unique voice, talent that could only be a gift of God, said that he relied on technique. With technique, he could sing through the times he was not in perfect health, still sound perfect and not injure his precious vocal chords.

You know you've mastered a step when you can do it properly when you are at your worst. You can be distracted, pressured, upset or ill, and still perform the task. You are not lost, flailing, stopping. You are relaxed and not second guessing yourself. You just do it, breathing easily. This is the benefit of a disciplined practice.

By the seventh month of karate class, the pain had begun. It stretched to eight years of debilitating illness with agonizing pain, undiagnosed until a hysterectomy when I was thirty-three revealed five different problems. Striving to heal myself through

33

karate's grueling physical, mental and emotional practice, I was in class every day for three to four hours, except the days when I was in fetal position screaming and throwing up. I didn't cure the illness, but I changed my life.

What would have happened if I had moved forward on the premise that I would not survive? Thankfully, I am courageous. As a child, I rode horses. My first horse was a beautiful black Welsh pony with white socks to her knees and a white snip on her nose. She enjoyed throwing my cousin Beth and me into the

Crisis is in the present; you can handle it step by step with clarity.

marshy little lakes that formed during the spring in the foothills of California. My last horse was a tall thoroughbred jumper. He was both extremely well-trained and extremely difficult to handle. Because I was afraid of him, I rode him bareback in the fields, jumping randomly over hay bales. He was thin, with high withers. If you know horses, you know that I was uncomfortable riding him bareback, especially jumping.

That's how I handle fear. I jump on and jump in. Through bold decisions and beautiful risks, I let nothing stand in my way. "Do the next step cheerfully," I remind myself. "Whatever it takes."

During this illness, I earned my black belt on my first try, after only two-and-a-half years. I was so disciplined and precise that I was made the top teacher under the master after five years. I was in charge of all those big men, many of whom had been there for a long time. My gender and size were irrelevant; my dedication and skill mattered. When I could not participate fully after the abdominal surgery, Master Pai had me stand next to him during seminar, our most intensive training period, which included hours of sparring, and taught me to see. It was among the most valuable trainings ever.

While I was undergoing chemotherapy for colon cancer years later, I was still teaching classes. I traded in my black belt for the strap-on belt with a bag of chemo dripping into the titanium port in my chest. But I was still teaching, still going to class. I didn't stop. I just kept on trucking. I did the easier things, the things that are all about grounding and simplicity and directness.

Being in the habit of taking the time to learn it and do it right, being able to replicate success, takes you through the hard times by anchoring you to process. Process is inherently present-mind. Crisis is in the present; you can handle it step by step with clarity. Outcome is in the future, where doubt and fear live. Having a grounded practice makes you feel more secure, so that you honor

---

The good practice is one that
makes you feel strengthened.

---

where you stand and always come from truth—an *authentic* premise. Start from the simple precept of honoring where you stand and then take the first step. Every step you take will move you ahead.

In martial arts, as in business and in life, we start at the beginning. Start with the foot positions, the stances, then move through the stances, like walking. Literally. Start with where you are, with your feet, and then move in the simplest way. Learn to take a stand and then take a step.

Even when you walk into a wall, you find out, "Oh, there's a wall in that direction!" So no matter what, you're getting information with every step. Paying attention as intimately as one does, as I certainly do and as I teach others to do, in each breath, in each step of martial arts, provides you a secure, honest foundation from which to pursue any path toward success. Be grounded; feel your breath, feel the soles of your feet. So if the earth shakes underneath you, however horrified you may be, you're not disabled.

For a while at the martial arts school, I was the only woman out of about forty students. I had seen a woman brown belt, but never a woman black belt. I entered that territory alone. Others followed me. Today the three top black belts under me are women.

The men were generally big, strong and aggressive. We had artists, writers and film makers, but also tough guys from Brooklyn, weightlifters, manual laborers, drug dealers, even a reputed hit man. Some were fine and behaved normally with me, bowing respectfully if I connected with a kick or punch. Others were macho with chips on their shoulders. Those men would punish me for being good, strong, aggressive, successful. They would come in with their strength, deliberately seeking to hurt me, to put me in my place. A few even touched my breasts or rear to insult me and get me flustered. It didn't work too well. My older brothers, each a foot taller than me, had tormented me from birth and made me pretty good at dealing with harassment.

While it may be unpopular to say that I cannot compete with men on size, innate strength and aggressiveness, that is my experience. I am five-foot, three-inches tall, was dealing with

Sometimes the hero's journey
requires becoming a warrior.

illness for the first eight years of practice and am reasonably nice. I have found that I gain more by developing other skills— precision, pragmatism, "no-mind" awareness and response— than by trying to compete with someone else's skill set. I stand where I am; I do not move forward on a false premise.

I have only met one person more precise than me—Rivers, the top student when I started, to whom I was apprenticed as I trained to take over his position, the first person I kicked in the balls. Rivers bowed and droned "Good kick, Campora." I have met only one person with greater understanding of our system and practice than I have, Grand Master Min Pai. He, Rivers and Grand Master William Cheung are the three I have personally met who are better martial artists than I am. I have met many people, all men, who are stronger, better fighters than I am.

When I met Mohammed Ali, he asked if I could whup the average man. I replied, "Not if the average man were like you, sir, but the *average* average man, why yes, I believe so."

Crises come up everywhere. You cannot know how to do everything. You can, however, know how to approach everything. When you have a relaxed, grounded body, your mind has a chance to function and figure it out. Today I was told I have early stage glaucoma. I made the follow-up appointment immediately, got the name of the best medication and am looking into my prescription insurance, which I will upgrade for optimum coverage. While not thrilled, I am not thrown off.

Begin your practice by standing, honoring where you stand. From there, from this place of truth, you can find a grounded practice from a grounded place. Maybe you haven't had a practice of grounding, but you do recognize when you feel solid or when you feel as though you're leaning over the precipice, when you feel strengthened or when you feel that the other person is so strong, stronger than you.

The good practice is one that makes you feel strengthened, not one that makes you feel gaga over a guru or the message they impart. Remember: There is no true conclusion from a false premise. Be impressed with yourself doing whatever it is, rather than impressed with others doing it. Look in the mirror and say, "I'm doing this for me. This is how I feel, not how somebody tells me to feel."

Sometimes the hero's journey requires becoming a warrior. The path to becoming a warrior begins with grounded practice. In business, in life; as you travel, as you grow; as you climb, as you reach, practice honoring where you stand, and then take a step.

Carolyn Campora is Master at Nabi Su Tai Chi, Kung Fu & Wellness, where she and fellow black belts teach students how to employ physical, mental and energetic techniques to calm and strengthen, expand awareness and enhance well-being. A practitioner of martial arts for more than forty years, Carolyn brings her training, wisdom and expertise to her students and clients.

Carolyn received her MBA in finance from Cornell University, did graduate-level art studies at New York Studio School of Drawing, Painting & Sculpture and received her Reiki Master Certification from Ibiki Ken Institute. She is an Accredited Level II Practitioner of Resonance Repatterning and a member of the Resonance Repatterning Practitioners' Association.

In addition to teaching Tai Chi and Kung Fu, Carolyn maintains a practice in several energy-based therapies, offering private sessions in Reiki, Resonance Repatterning® and astrology, guiding clients as they evolve in well-being and fulfillment. Carolyn also offers Executive Wellness programs for corporations, a fast track to stress reduction and improved productivity.

Carolyn is the author of Bunnoidity, *a charming philosophical book for adults and children (www.BunnyPrintsBooks.com). She is currently writing a series of martial arts books. Connect with Carolyn at www.NabiSu.com.*

Now Is the Time to Harvest

I t was a few days before the New Year when my sister called and said that she needed to talk with me. There was something about the way she said it. Somehow I knew this "talk" would be different from the many other talks we'd had over a lifetime of being sisters and the past twenty years of me managing her and her music career. That night I tossed and turned, blankets bunched up around my legs, unable to ignore the nagging feeling that something was very wrong.

The next day, I went to my sister's house. The combined scents of pine, patchouli and sandalwood intensified as I made my way up to the third floor. Over the years, I had come to associate those scents with my sister. She loves her candles!

When I saw her face, her detached expression and slightly somber disposition confirmed that I was quite right in sensing there was something wrong. We hugged, kissed, made a little small talk. Then, in her classic, get-to-the-point style, she cut right to the chase. "Tammy, I'm going to get a new manager."

She might as well have said, "Tammy, your life is over. Done!" With those eight words, my identity vanished.

All of my life I have been referred to as "Chaka Khan's sister," and for twenty years I had been referred to as "Chaka's sister and manager." "Tammy," the name that she gave Mom for me when I was born, ironically became secondary to the title, "Chaka's sister and manager." That identity was so ingrained in me that I too made the needs, desires and priorities of "Tammy" secondary to fulfilling my role as "Chaka's sister and manager."

I was numb. In the past when this topic came up (and it did on several occasions), I would boldly shoot it down with a *that ain't happenin'* attitude backed by my confidence in my abilities. I knew I was the best person for the job, and that was the end of that! Not this time.

"I met with another manager. We're meeting again in another week or so," Chaka said. Suddenly, I became terrified for her. I thought, *If she's solely looked at as a commodity, will she suffer the fate of so many of her contemporaries?* That was my *real* job—to protect her. Not just protect her physical well-being, but also her integrity as an artist. Who would protect her? It involved so much more than the day-to-day management of her professional career.

---

*I had been living with feelings
of betrayal for months. Now I
understood: I was the betrayer.*

"Will you at least interview other managers before you make a decision? I'll help with the process," I said. She agreed. We hugged. She asked me if I was okay, and I lied and said, "Yes." The journey down those stairs and out to my car began my journey to Tammy, deep down into Tammy. There was no place else to go.

As I pulled into my driveway, I could hear my son, Tallon, screaming. Now sixteen, he was diagnosed with autism at the age of three. Tallon is generally mild-mannered and, to a great extent, nonverbal. Occasionally, and particularly on this night, he was "on one," as my husband Gil and I say. Yep, Tallon was definitely "on one." His younger brother—my thirteen-year-old son, Tyler

—and Ettie, our caretaker of ten years, were trying to calm him down. Tallon, who is nearly six feet tall and two hundred pounds, is not an easy one to tame when he gets into this rage. We can't seem to figure out what prompts it, except that he is intuitively sensitive to the energy around him. That night, he was certainly tuning into mine.

When I went to bed, I told Gil about the day, my tears soaking his shirt as I released the pain, fear and anxiety that consumed me. As I vented, it came to me that my sister had to have a co-conspirator. I knew Chaka. She wouldn't just call another manager for a meeting. *Who would betray me like this?* I thought. When I figured it out, I called my sister, and she confirmed it.

I became angry and resentful. Not just toward my sister, but toward those I felt had betrayed me by assisting in arranging this meeting. *I hired these people. I put forth energy and resources to help them with their own endeavors, and they have betrayed me like this!*

Gil and my best friend Veronica were the shoulders I leaned on when I felt weak and vulnerable. While most of my family held a space of love and support for Chaka and me through this transition, others gossiped about how she fired me without ever picking up the phone to see how I was doing. I know that it was shocking for most and awkward for others; each person reacted in his or her own unique way.

As I went through my grieving process, I was meeting almost daily with my sister, her business manager and her life coach. If we were not meeting about our transition, we were meeting with management candidates. I would initiate the interview process by assuring each potential manager that our decision to transition was mutual and that I was steering this process to assure that my sister was placed in good hands.

Although it started as the script, "the decision being mutual" slowly became my authentic truth. And coming to that truth was a slow process. These were very emotional times for me. It might have been easier had I been able to detach and move on, but I remained manager pro tem until we selected my replacement.

In one of our "transition" meetings, I was brimming with anger. I began to recall the countless occasions when I had to endure the embarrassment of my sister showing up high as a kite or not showing up at all. I thought about the sleepless nights and painstaking details that went into cueing up career-defining opportunities only to see her sabotage them in the eleventh hour.

In this meeting and in the heat of my anger, I turned to Chaka and said, "If it weren't for me, you wouldn't even be viable or relevant right now." That statement was harsh, but not as harsh as my thoughts: *After all, I am the one who journeyed with you through two rehab programs, the release of seventy-five pounds of excess weight and so much more! This is unfair! I invested my life in you!* My outburst was the epitome of an ego trip. It was mean. I was in deep pain and I wanted her to feel it too.

Mission accomplished. My words were painful. It was a real low blow, and she took it like a champ. Then, with much greater tact and empathy, she released some of her pain and resentment by letting me know that she actually resented me for doing for her what she should have done for herself. Our relationship was very co-dependent, and I was far too enabling. I didn't understand her resentment at first—until I realized that I too had the same resentment toward her. I resented her, because I was doing for her what I should have been doing for me. Hell, I didn't even know who I was!

Who was *I*? What did *I* want? I became an avid *Super Soul Sunday* watcher on the Oprah Winfrey Network and I faithfully tuned in to Joel Osteen and either live-streamed or attended Agape Church.

I also discovered the University of Santa Monica's spiritual psychology master's program and I read… a lot. Each of these methods supported me during this time and not only taught me to accept this change, but also renewed my faith and ignited my passion for the pursuit of my purpose.

In addition to these modes of spiritual edification, spinning became my sanctuary. A lot of my healing took place at spinning class, led by Angela at SoulCycle. I distinctly remember being on the bike and, more than likely triggered by something Angela said, becoming overwhelmed with gratitude for my sister. I

Our divine nature is to create, that is the
part of us that is made in His image.

---

started managing my sister when I was a baby. She trusted her then twenty-year career to my very enthusiastic, passionate and protective, yet green, hands. With Chaka I traveled the world; I have been to every continent on this planet except Antarctica. I've met the most amazing people and have had experiences that most have only dreamed about.

I literally felt about twenty pounds lighter when I got off of that bike. I couldn't wait to get home and write a letter to my sister expressing my gratitude. The letter ended with, "This season has ended. We've survived the winter. It's now time to harvest." And that is when my new journey began.

The simple practice of conscious breathing helped me connect with my higher self. More and more I began to see how alignment with my higher self, my *true self*, really is the path of least resistance. I could see that the universe really is conspiring on my behalf and for my highest good.

I began to practice trusting my intuition and my emotions as the guideposts for staying in alignment with Source, and as a result experienced the magic of Divine synchronicity. For me, it was keeping my vibration in the frequency of love and gratitude. When I stay there, I am a magnet for Divine manifestation.

When I find myself out of alignment, I tune into my emotions, acknowledge them, allow myself to feel them and then move back into love and gratitude.

I had been living with feelings of betrayal for months. Now I understood: I was the betrayer. I had betrayed myself. I stayed in way past the expiration date. As a single mom for eight years, I put my career before my children and let a nanny do for me what I should have been doing for them. I was not living an authentic life. I was not living my purpose. On many levels, respect between my sister and me had vanished because I lost respect for myself.

The anger and resentment that I had for the so-called "co-conspirators" was transmuted to love and gratitude through this process. For some time, I couldn't converse with them. It wasn't until I went through the emotions that were present for me and had arrived in a place of gratitude that I could reach out in love

------

*As my purpose became clear, I
began to see my life become what
I call divinely synchronized.*

------

and honestly thank them for the role that they played. And I did. I called each one of them and thanked them. *Whew! Another twenty pounds lifted,* I thought. *I'm catching up to my sister's weight loss. Now I just need it to manifest in the physical world!*

During a business lunch, Laura, a new business associate at the time, invited me to her home in Aspen for a spiritual retreat. I spontaneously accepted the invitation trusting that the Universe would support me being able to fulfill the commitment. The next thing I knew I was on a plane, ascending above the clouds, flying over Colorado's snowcapped mountains and descending to the Aspen Airport. My flight was quite a metaphor for the experience I was about to embark on: piercing through the clouds of fear and doubt and having a shift in perspective; what I once perceived as an arduous mountain to climb I now viewed from an aerial perspective. I could now see a direct and clear path to TAMMY.

I began pursuing my personal development "bucket list." I started taking classes online at a Christian university. One of my class assignments was to write an essay about visiting a church. I had to interview the pastor of the church for the essay as well. I chose Agape Church and Reverend Michael Beckwith. I ended up getting an "A" on the essay and in the class. However, my highest honor was giving Reverend Beckwith a copy of my essay and having him share it with the congregation on Easter Sunday.

Reverend Beckwith commented on the fact that it was well written, and he shared the commentary from my professor.

By being love and expressing gratitude,
you give others permission to do the same.

Reverend Michael Bernard Beckwith, who's been featured in the film *The Secret*, interviewed by Oprah Winfrey and Larry King, one of today's most enlightened spiritual teachers, featured as a guest alongside the Dalai Lama, quoted me! This was one of the first validations of my gift as a writer. I was starting to discover "TAMMY."

My mornings started in meditation and prayer. Then I read. Usually, I read a few books at the same time. I was really getting into a nice place. I became more confident, had greater peace and was narrowing in on purpose.

A couple of years ago, I reserved a website domain called "Artistology." I didn't quite know what I was going to use it for, but I loved the word and couldn't believe that it was available. If you break down the etymology of the word "Artistology," "Artist" means "one who creates," and "ology" is "the study of." I've always had a love and respect for the artist, the creator, that part of us that is made in God's image. In that respect, we are all artists.

Our divine nature is to create; that is the part of us that is made in His image.

Performing artists, in my opinion, have a greater responsibility to maintain integrity in their creations because they are messengers. They are messengers on a mass level. William S. Burroughs said it best: "Artists to my mind are the real architects of change, and not the political legislators who implement change after the fact." This is evidenced by the fact that there is a direct correlation between the state of a society and the music, film and television programs that are created in it. *What kind of world could we manifest if more artists took on this responsibility?*

There it was! My purpose is to empower artists to align with their higher selves so that they can in turn inspire others to do the same. ARTISTOLOGY™ was born with the mission of "Empowering you so that you can empower the world!"

As my purpose became clear, I began to see my life become what I call divinely synchronized. I practiced following my intuition. I listened to that quiet voice and followed it. I trusted it. Each and every time, the resources and support would be there to confirm that I was in alignment.

In retrospect, I see that my intuition told me the conversation that my sister and I were to have would change the trajectory of my life and our relationship. My intuition also told me that Reverend Beckwith was going to share my paper on Easter Sunday. My intuitive nature has always been there; I just wasn't attuned to it before. As Reverend Beckwith, in his analogous style of teaching, shared once in a sermon: we energetically vibrate at various frequencies, like a radio, and depending on which frequency we are vibrating we tune in to the information and circumstances that match it. As I became aligned with my higher Self, I tuned in to my intuitive nature.

The fear that once immobilized me and kept me thinking, doing and saying "the right thing" or "the safe thing" has lost its power. I now live and speak my truth (which is love!) more and more each day.

Betrayal, loss, major transitions that leave you wondering who you are—welcome them. By being love and expressing gratitude, you give others permission to do the same. It's so liberating. It's so empowering. You just have to have the courage and the faith to "survive the winter."

TAMMY is an author, speaker, and empowerment retreat facilitator. She has twenty-seven years experience in the entertainment industry, and is the co-founder and CEO of ARTISTOLOGY™. ARTISTOLOGY™ facilitates empowerment retreats guided by practitioners that are spirit led. Through the ARTISTOLOGY™ method of coaching, clients connect with their authentic Self, align with their creative gifts and talents and pursue their purpose with passion. Connect with TAMMY at www.Artistology.com.

Deborah Bateman

The Flame Within

My first day of work at my dream job in New York City, I walked the few blocks to my new office building as if on a cloud. It was a beautiful, crisp, January morning, and I was grateful for my boots and my long, cashmere coat—new wardrobe pieces that were foreign to me in my home state of Arizona.

Entering the front doors of our headquarters, my sense of pride swelled. *This is where I belong,* I thought. After more than thirty years in the banking industry, having survived multiple mergers and acquisitions, I felt ready to join the ranks of senior management and take on the major project for which I had been promoted.

I saw my new position as validation of the value I could create for my bank. The job meant so much that I had convinced my husband of twenty-four years that we should divorce and split our financial assets, so I could move to Manhattan to continue my career, and we could remain "transcontinental friends."

Our daughter, Tara, was grown and both of us were living our own lives; for months Tim and I had discussed how we should handle our split. It was the easiest divorce I'd ever heard of—it ended amicably, and we remained friends, with the promise of seeing each other whenever I was in town. It was time for me to come into my own, to live the life I was meant for; and even if Tim had been resistant to the idea, it would not have stopped me from taking the job.

Once I was inside the building, the metal detectors gave me pause. It was 2003, not long after the tragedy of 9/11, and New York had changed. It seemed everyone I met had known someone who perished in the World Trade Center's Twin Towers.

As I approached the security check-in, I placed my briefcase and purse on the conveyor belt and showed the security officer my ID badge. Clearing security, I gathered my belongings and

*I felt ready to join the ranks
of senior management.*

rode the elevators that would take me to my floor. I savored the feeling of going up, thinking about my future career and my own personal success. With every fiber of my being, I was thrilled.

The doors opened on the forty-seventh floor to reveal a stunning lobby—quiet, clean, professional and recently decorated. When I introduced myself at the reception desk, an attractive woman stood up and extended her hand. "Welcome, Ms. Bateman," she said. "We've been expecting you. Would you like me to show you to your office?"

I was giddy. *I'm going to love working here,* I thought. *This is exactly how I imagined it.* Following the receptionist through the corridors to my office, I caught a glimpse of my name on the wall next to my door. *Deborah Bateman. Yes, they had been expecting me.*

My office took my breath away—gray marble floors, plush carpeting the color of amethyst, a modern, birds-eye maple desk and wall unit accented with thick glass desktop and shelves. Large windows provided real-time artwork. To my right, I could see the Empire State Building high above the other office buildings; to my left, the exquisite Chrysler building with its Art Deco design was my view. As I looked directly west, I could see the Hudson River. Working in this magnificent city with the financial leaders of our banking industry was my dream, my goal, my aspiration for so many years. I had made it.

"Is there anything I can get you?" the receptionist said, interrupting my thoughts. "Would you like a cup of coffee?"

"No thanks," I replied. "I just want to get moved in. Thank you so much."

Near the window, on a small conference table, someone had placed everything I would need to get started at my new job: boxes and bags of office supplies, a laptop and a medium-sized bright orange drawstring bag branded with the bank's logo.

I was staring at a gas mask!

I opened the bag. Inside I found a lanyard with a whistle—*I can put my new ID card on this; how handy!*—a folded, laminated map of the forty-seventh floor and... a flashlight? *Hmm. Why do I need a flashlight?*

Feeling around in the bag, I pulled out one more item, which was wrapped in tissue. When I tore away the tissue, my breath caught and my chest tightened. I was staring at a gas mask! In an instant, my excitement was gone. I felt like a balloon deflating. All that wonderful energy from the morning rushed out of my body as I realized that this bright orange bag was an emergency kit. A *survival* kit. Again, I looked out my windows at my gorgeous view and this time, my eyes focused on the space where the World Trade Center had stood. Suddenly, an incredible panic seized my body.

What the heck have I done? I'm standing on the forty-seventh floor of a global financial institution, in a city targeted by terrorists! What the hell am I doing here?

In that moment, all my core values became very clear. I had made the wrong decision. My dream, which I had been chasing, was an illusion. Why would I want to trade what I had once had for the realities of life in Manhattan?

I felt an overwhelming need to get out—out of the building, out of the neighborhood, out of New York City altogether. But there was no way I could leave. I was in charge of an important and highly visible project. More importantly, I had dedicated my life to this industry and had worked hard to climb the corporate ladder, providing value at every step. I had made material sacrifices, even given up my marriage and my Arizona home, to pursue this goal.

Over the next year, I worked twelve to fourteen-hour days. In my off time, I thought long and hard about how I ended up in this situation. Every month or so, I would fly back to Arizona to see Tara and Tim. When we ended our marriage, I had said to him, "A piece of paper isn't going to commit us to each other. We'll always be friends. We'll visit each other." It all seemed so simple at the time, but it was anything but.

My dream, which I had been chasing, was an illusion.

A few months after my move to New York City, Tim said, "Deborah, I can't continue to do this. I can't have you go away for a month, live your own life, and then come back to see me and pretend that everything is the same. I can't do this."

I could see that Tim was struggling, and my heart went out to him. Still, I did not expect the next words to come out of his mouth: "I don't want to see you or talk to you anymore."

"You don't mean that," I said.

"I do mean it," Tim replied, his voice tinged with sadness.

Stunned, the only reply I could come up with was, "If you change your mind, call me."

Out of respect for Tim, I stopped all contact with him. In the months that followed, I came to recognize that, while attempting to prioritize a successful career, I had lost myself and potentially had lost some of the most important components of my life. In addition, I couldn't quantify, to myself, the value I was creating in my current position. Ultimately, I realized that I didn't know myself that well and that I needed to know myself. So, I resigned.

I took a year off to explore and find answers to my questions: What do I want my life to be? How can I make a real difference in the world? What makes me happy?

Moving back to Arizona was an easy decision. I came back to Phoenix with no corporate job title, as a divorced and single woman; and, even though I was still a mother, Tara was grown,

Never again would I find myself
caught up in an all-consuming job.

traveling the world and pursuing her own career, and I was unemployed. In finding myself, I was starting with a "blank piece of paper."

Not knowing where to begin, I started with many of the things that a career woman like myself never had time to do. I took cooking classes. I learned to appreciate wine. I planted an herb garden. I traveled. I bought a home and decorated it myself. I renewed my commitment to philanthropic projects and mentorship of others. Slowly, by listening to the voice in my heart, I found myself. The *real* me.

By the time I was ready to go back to work, I knew who I was. I sought an organization whose core values aligned with mine and approached them. I talked about the value I could contribute to their company. And I also told them what I was willing to do, and what I was *not* willing to do. Never again would I find myself caught up in an all-consuming job.

When Tara suffered a minor injury, I reached out to Tim for the first time since our final conversation. I informed him of Tara's injury; I let him know she was fine, but that she would need time to recover. I said, "I think as parents it would be best if we unite in case she needs us."

Tim was very closed off when he stopped by my house to see Tara. But after talking with her for over an hour, he came to me and said, "Can you show me your home?"

Playing tour guide, I was proud to show him the art and furniture I had purchased. He said, "Deborah, your home is absolutely beautiful. In fact, you've done a few things I probably would have objected to when we were married."

His words were like magic to me. When Tim said that, I realized that I had truly broken free from the person he wanted me to be and who my employer wanted me to be. I had become a full expression of my authentic self.

That day was a beginning for Tim and me. We started talking again, reconnecting on a new level, as whole people. We rediscovered each other and fell in love again. We were remarried

Are you defining yourself by your own terms?

in 2006, three years after our divorce. We call the time we spent apart a "correction" in our marriage. Would we feel the way we feel about each other now—as though we're soul mates, so in love—if we had stayed married thirty consecutive years? Probably not—*unless* I would have had the self-awareness and the courage to get to know myself, to find myself, and unless we had each sought our own truth within the confines of our marriage.

Today, I define myself not by the success I sacrificed for in the past, but by the way I feel inside. There is a flame in your upper chest, near your heart. When I am living authentically, mine burns. I can feel the fire; I can feel the passion. *That's* how I know I'm on the right path.

As you walk toward your dream job, or stand in the elevator waiting to be let off at the place you've been working toward for months, years, or even decades, ask yourself the important questions: Are you defining yourself by your own terms? Or, are you allowing others to impose their expectations on you? Are you wrapped up in an idea or a goal that is in true alignment with what you truly value most in life? Or, are you trying to be the person your parents, your significant other, your children or your employers expect you to be?

Listen to your heart. Are you reaching for the right dreams? Are you pushing for the right reasons? The answers are within. The truth of who you are burns there. Can you feel it?

Deborah Bateman is Vice Chairman of the board of directors for a statewide bank in Phoenix, Arizona. Deborah is involved with the ongoing development of the bank, with a focus on the bank's impact and engagement in the Arizona communities. A veteran banker, Deborah's career has spanned leadership capacities throughout banking. Deborah is a graduate of Mesa Community College, Pacific Coast Banking School at the University of Washington and Darden's Leadership Development Program at the University of Virginia.

An active member of the community, Deborah currently serves on the Board of Directors for The O'Connor House, Florence Crittendon, Arizona Council for Economic Education, GPD American Heart Association, The Patrick Peterson Foundation and the Phoenix Suns Charities. In addition, Deborah is a member of Charter 100, Women Presidents' Organization, Central Phoenix Women, ASU's Women and Philanthropy, Arizona 5 Arts Council and the Heart Ball.

Deborah has been recognized in the community in numerous ways. Some of the more significant recognition includes: Stevie Award —Best Executive in the Financial Services Industry Award, Cancer Support Community Hope Award, Girl Scouts of America Women of Distinction—Leadership Award, AZ Business magazine—50 Most Influential Women in Arizona Business, and The National Association of Women Business Owners Visionary Award.

Today, Deborah shares her experience as a mentor, speaker and world traveler with individuals, corporations and community groups alike. Connect with Deborah at www.DeborahBateman.com.

Michèle Gunderson, PhD

Just Focus Here

I am standing in the hallway at SAIT, back against the wall. My whole body is shaking, and I can feel that place in my throat where the breath won't come. The tears feel as if they are stuffed up there, right in my throat. I will not cry. My face is tight, eyes stinging. My chest feels like lead and the back of my neck aches. Oh please, not again. It's been years. I thought I was through with this. Yet here we go again….

My Aikido instructor has followed me outside the class. He can smell fear, and mine is visceral, coursing through my body in waves.

The fear has no reality to it. No one is going to hurt me, least of all the small-framed and affable man who is my ex-husband, who recently decided to take the martial arts class my thirteen-year-old daughter and I are taking. It is his second class, and I am bursting. This man has never hit me, never laid a hand on me. Of course not. He is not that kind of man. He has raised money for the heart fund. He is a musician and an engineer, loved at his job. He is a good father.

And I am outside in the hallway, shaking. Thoughts race through my mind: *Is it because I am afraid he will hurt me? Or is it that I'm afraid some part of me wants to hurt him? Maybe*

I have somehow unconsciously taken this class to defend myself against him—and now he's here and he is supposed to throw me to the mat, and I cannot move.

Outside in the hallway, my instructor tries to get me to look in his eyes. He is saying something. I can't hear his words. But I feel his presence, his body near mine. He is over six feet tall, solid as a rock. I sense his protectiveness, his strength.

My daughter is still in class. I need to pull myself together.

I teach breath work in my yoga classes, and still I can't breathe. I teach people to find their own stories in the writing workshops I facilitate. *Where is my story now?* It's as if the earth has fallen out from beneath me and swallowed me whole.

"Focus," he says. "Just focus."

When we finally go back in, he lets the other instructor continue the class, and he takes me on as his private student that day.

"Look in my eyes. Look here," he says, and then says it again.

I am outside in the hallway, shaking.

"Here, focus here." My eyes drift over to the man across the room, and the instructor puts his hand on my face and draws my focus back again. "Look here."

He takes me through each motion, one small bit at a time. I can't think. I can barely hear his words. But he has me glue my eyes to him and repeat the motions, over and over. This man who trains people in deadly combat out on the grassy fields of Calgary in his spare time, whose martial arts training extends far beyond the self-defensive postures of Aikido, who hides knives around his house and who could kill me with one swift move—this man actually makes me feel safe.

Here. Just focus here.

As I drove home afterward, something my oldest friend said to me once years ago echoed through my mind. It happened at my parent's cabin, my then-small daughter playing quietly in the next room. My friend and I had been sitting on the bed together, sobbing quietly so my daughter wouldn't hear.

I had poured my heart out to her, crazy with grief over my whole messed-up life. It wasn't supposed to be this way. We talked and talked, and yet I only remember one thing she said: "He's made you forget how beautiful you are."

She had known me since I was four. You can't fool someone who watched you pick your nose and who dressed up with you

---

*How had my own story become
so buried, so lost?*

---

in play wedding gowns for that perfect day. She knew. She saw me. She was right.

Driving home, I thought of her words. "He's made you forget how beautiful you are."

But it wasn't that he had done it. My friend was finding kind words to support me in the crisis of the arguments and the fear, the trips to counseling and the quiet advice to find a safe place to run to, just in case. Yes, bad stuff was happening. But he hadn't done it. What I realized that day, driving home from Aikido, was that I'd done it to myself.

I'd let myself forget. I'd forgotten how capable I was, how much I had to offer, how deeply I could serve this planet. And that's what hurt the most. I had lost my own story and replaced it with the stories of others. Whose stories had I listened to? How had my own story become so buried, so lost?

Teaching at the university for years, I had been nominated for a teaching award by my students. So many of them came back to me years later to tell me that in four years of university, mine was the best class they'd taken—they all told me that I was the one who had taught them to write. Then, leaving the university to teach people how to breathe through yoga, I became one of the most highly certified Iyengar yoga teachers in my city and now had years of intensive training behind me.

How had I lost it all? What had happened to me?

The month after that Aikido class, I made a decision. I registered for a year-long mastermind that cost twenty thousand dollars. I wanted to be around others who were moving their lives forward, who were taking chances, taking

------

*Change my story, take a
step, change my life.*

------

care of themselves and this planet no matter what. Since my ex-husband had always been the one who made the money and he'd left me over a year earlier, this was a crazy move. But I had made a decision. I would not stand outside, back to the wall, letting life pass me by.

I had mentored others; hundreds, probably thousands had already been touched by my work. Their lives were changing. *What about mine?*

One decision, a leap of faith: Change my story, take a step, change my life. And my life started changing so rapidly it made my head spin. From making less than two hundred dollars in my business the whole month after that day at Aikido, I found myself less than a year later bringing home thirty-two thousand in just over a month in my business. It was a miracle, one that started with a simple thought, a decision.

Focus here. Right here.

I knew I had to root out those fears that were coming back and freezing me to the wall, sucking the life out of me. I needed to own my body, and my life, once again. And I needed support.

Now I offer that support to my students, and the results have been incredible. I teach three week-long retreats a year in the Canadian Rockies, the Gulf Islands and along the coast of Mexico. I have a year-long "Love Your Words, Love Your Life" community where I help my students find the beauty in their own lives, their own stories. And I help them find the words to say it.

Most of all, through finding their stories, I help them stop stopping themselves so that they can finally live the lives they're meant to live. I don't want anyone on this planet to find that someone else's story has become lodged in their body, so that they're sent to the hospital, or worse.

So many creative women are out there, and men too, whose stories are blocked in ways they don't even know. Some of the writers I work with have had stories stuck inside them for thirty

---

Focus, just focus. Here. Here.

---

years. I help them find a way to tell their own story. Whether they're writing a blog post, a novel, a speech, a memoir, a short story or copy for their website, I help them to be heard.

I want all their stories to be heard. I help my students root out the unhelpful stories and find the stories that have always been there for them.

Focus, just focus. Here. Here.

Then leap, and the net will appear.

This is your story.

It is your birthright.

Here. Now.

Begin.

Michèle Gunderson, PhD, inspires her students to discover and delight in their own innate creativity. She is the founder of The Language of Yoga, a company that helps both new and experienced writers stop the inner chatter, end procrastination and negative self-talk, and win the inner game of writing—and of life.

An Iyengar yoga teacher and former university professor, Michèle draws on the ancient wisdom of yoga and on cutting-edge writing techniques to allow her students' writing to flourish in completely new ways. Her mission is to inspire millions to allow their writing— and their lives—to flow with ease, so they can discover their own authentic voice and powerfully share their stories with the world. Connect with Michèle at www.MicheleGunderson.com.

Di Riseborough

The Other F-Word

In 2007, twelve years after the horrific tragedy that forever changed my family, I returned to my native South Africa to face the man who murdered my grandmother.

After setting up a meeting through the warden, I borrowed a car and set out on the two-hour journey from my mom's house to the prison. The whole way there I felt really calm; I had no thoughts, no expectations. Since I arrived an hour early, I sat in a coffee shop with a little journal, intending to write down questions to ask my grandmother's killer. "What do I want to say to him?" I asked myself. Again, nothing came.

Instead, the memories of what happened came flooding back. Hearing the news that my paternal grandmother had been violently murdered was a devastating shock. Even more unbelievable was the discovery that my uncle's estranged wife, Susan, had been behind the plan to kill her mother-in-law—and that her own son, a young man whom we called Wolfe, whom my grandmother loved as her own, was the perpetrator. Years of dealing with overwhelming grief and rage; the desire for revenge. My family's inability to cope; my own feelings of powerlessness and betrayal. It all came back in pictures, in echoes of emotions I'd worked hard to release over years of focused practice.

After spinning out of control for two years, I had moved to Canada to create a new life for myself and heal the pain from the past. I took workshops and learned how to work with energy. I found someone who could help me understand my emotions. After the trial, I was afraid to deal with my anger, concerned that if I let my rage out I would not be able to stop and I might hurt myself or somebody else.

I learned how to calm myself down, how to release anger and other emotions in healthy ways and how to be present in my mind and body. Connecting my mind with body and spirit, I began to become aware of and understand what was happening in my body, and through that, trust my emotions. I was ready to face the past and the man who had set my downward spiral in motion.

When it was almost time for my appointed meeting, I made my way to the prison. Driving up to the dusty gate, I noticed a few prisoners standing in the garden. I was surprised to find that, despite the barbed wire fence, the building wasn't frightening at all. Once inside, a woman at a desk greeted me, took my bag and notified the deputy warden I had arrived.

I returned to my native South Africa to face the man who murdered my grandmother.

It was only when I went to use the bathroom that I broke into tears. It had been building for weeks, ever since I made the decision to visit Wolfe. My intention in coming to see him had nothing to do with him; it was about healing myself and confirming that all of the work I'd committed to doing was real and effective.

In November, just before my trip back home to South Africa, I had finished another piece of release of emotion. When that was completed, I felt a total relief in my body. My heart exploded. It may sound flaky and weird, but ever since I was a child I've been intuitive; I'm able to sense people, even those who are far away.

Not long after I released my last piece of anger and resentment, Susan's face started coming into my consciousness. I'd be driving my car and she would come to mind. In the past, just the mention of her name would incite rage as my body reacted negatively. I was angrier with Susan than I was with Wolfe, because she got off without having to face justice. And yet now, when I thought of her, I had no reaction.

For a week, Susan came to me and then, toward the end, faded slowly. I knew I had to see Wolfe. Looking in the mirror in the prison bathroom, I remembered thinking, *It's time for me to have the courage to go back. I'm in a good space and I want to tell him how his actions impacted my life.*

We all have a contract to learn a lesson.

After I wiped my face with a tissue, I walked with two guards down the corridor to the deputy warden's office. Surrounded by bookshelves in his khaki-colored office, by walls made of cement brick, I chatted with the deputy. Finally I asked, "Does Wolfe seem to have any remorse?"

"Not in the beginning, no," he replied. "But since he lost his mother, I've seen a change in him."

I was stunned to find out Susan had passed away. "When did she die?" I asked.

"Around Christmas."

I recalled the week Susan came to mind every day and thought about the profound healing in my heart and wondered, *Who released whom? Did she die and release me? Or did I release her, and then she died?*

While I waited for Wolfe to arrive, I sat quietly in the office and reflected on this news. *Another gift has been given to me here.* In this world, we are all connected. We all have a contract to learn a lesson, and my lesson is to learn compassion to that degree and forgiveness to that degree. You learn by doing, by going through experience. You have to do the work, but in the end you have been given the gift of the lesson.

And then all too quickly, there he was. In his orange jumpsuit, too big for his slight frame, Wolfe looked the same. Nothing much had changed, except he was thinner, the physical impact of living in prison. Somehow I thought he would grow into a big man, but he seemed smaller, and timid.

We sat on opposite sides of the room, the two guards off to one side to give us as much privacy as possible. We exchanged hellos. He asked me where I lived. I'm not sure what made me do it, but I got up, crossed the room and sat down right next to him. I could tell Wolfe was afraid, but I felt I had to be near him. I felt no fear.

Nothing changes unless you are
willing to face your fears.

Sitting shoulder to shoulder, Wolfe started to explain what happened on that terrible day. He talked for a long time, and to this day I can't recall what he said. It wasn't important; I wasn't there to hear his side of the story. It didn't matter. I had come for another purpose.

When he was finished, I said, "I want to tell you what happened to my family."

Wolfe tensed up, but he listened as I told him how his actions basically destroyed us, that we had lost so much more than my grandmother that day. In a calm voice I said, "You know my uncle died soon after you killed her. Well, two years later, my father passed away. His health was ravaged by his inability to cope with what happened. And my mother—she's never recovered from finding grandmother's body. She still has nightmares every night."

Emotional but calm, I summoned up my courage and went on to explain the impact this senseless murder had on my own life—

how much anger I had had toward him and his mother, and the years of feeling helpless and out of control. Finally, I said, "You also took away my trust. Not just my trust in people. You took away my trust in humanity."

We were silent for a moment, and then I asked, "Was it worth it?"

"No. I'm so sorry, Diane."

Without hesitation I turned to him and said, "I've forgiven you."

He seemed surprised. "I can't forgive myself."

"You have to forgive yourself. It's the only way you can move forward."

Wolfe shook his head ever so slightly and in a quiet voice said, "I don't think I'll be able to do that."

Wolfe wasn't ready to consider releasing any of the pain, shame or regret he carried. In my own healing work and in my healing work with clients, I've learned that you cannot run away from your life—it's there every day when you wake up. You can avoid, deny

---

Don't give into your anxiety about
starting the forgiveness process.

---

and distract yourself, you can wear your mask, but eventually the Universe will create a situation where you are forced to look at it. Nothing changes unless you are willing to face your fears, until you have the courage to do the work.

Life throws us curveballs, and yes, bad things happen to good people. But we have an inner spirit that is resilient and we only have one life to live. When we get knocked down we get up and heal; we find the courage to face our fears, our shame, and it is imperative we deal with our emotions, as they are the sign posts of what needs healing. Staying stuck in your head will not change anything. The connection between the mind and body needs to be made, so you can live from your soulful purpose and not what the ego/monkey mind creates for you. When we change our inner world, our external world also starts to change for the better.

Walking out of the prison that day was a surreal moment. I kept thinking, *Is this real? What have I done?* It felt so big. And I felt so different. I sat in my car for a while before I drove back; I knew I would be inundated with questions from my family and I wanted to sit with my feelings. I waited for the anger I knew so well and had lived with for so long to come back, but there was nothing. There was only peace. I felt as though I was floating. For nearly half an hour I sat there in a blissful state of lightness and joy. *I'm free.* I smiled all the way home.

Forgiveness is the foundation of creating happiness in your life. When you forgive someone, or yourself, you reclaim your power. The act of forgiveness is you taking it back. And until you find the inner courage to forgive, you will be stuck, a part of you lost to the

---

*You can make the choice to find the
courage to reclaim your power.*

---

person or situation you cannot release. I had the courage to face Wolfe and my fears. I had the courage to heal. We all have that; the spark is within all of us and we just have to make the flame bigger. You may think you don't have the courage, but you do.

Lately I've had a lot of clients who are business owners and I notice that the main thing they struggle with is self-forgiveness. They can't figure out why they are struggling in their businesses, not realizing it's in part because they are not connected to their emotional selves and how that relates to their businesses. Entrepreneurs are often head people, caught up in the monkey mind. From that place, the forgiveness process seems daunting.

Don't give into your anxiety about starting the forgiveness process. It's not easy, but it's not as hard as we make it out to be.

When you release the pain and shame and anger and resentment, you will experience a peace you have never known before. And when you find inner peace, your outer world will begin to shift and present you with boundless opportunities for connection, fulfillment and joy.

Realize there is a lesson in what is happening to you, and part of that experience is how you handle it. You can continue to avoid your emotions and remain disconnected from your body and spirit; you can continue to blame and hide and rage and suffer. Or you can empower yourself to take control of your life. You can make the choice to find the courage to reclaim your power.

Before I left the prison that day, Wolfe asked, "May I give you a gift?"

I agreed. He left with a guard and came back with a card on which he had drawn a picture of a butterfly on a flower. Inside the card he had written, "Thank you for coming to see me. Thank you for helping me." In that moment I could feel all of this healing happening; the energy was everywhere in the room.

He turned to leave, but before he could I stopped the guard and asked, "May I give him a hug?"

Wolfe looked hesitant. I had never hugged him as a kid; I only saw him once or twice a year. When the guard agreed, I stepped forward and wrapped my arms around Wolfe. It felt as though I had grown, as though I had gotten so big energetically. Engulfing him in a bear hug, I felt a warmth flow into my heart. I could feel him shaking.

I held him while he cried, my body, my mind, my spirit, my everything so full of compassion and love for this man who had taken away someone very dear to me, for this man upon whom I once dreamt of exacting revenge. As he sobbed in my arms I said, "Please, *please* forgive yourself."

Please forgive *yourself*. It's time.

Di Riseborough is a transformational speaker, author and intuitive life strategist, featured on the Oprah Winfrey Network. Through her work, she has helped thousands of people use the "F-word" more effectively in their lives, learn to face unresolved fears and discover how to forgive themselves and others. Through her own powerful story of forgiving the man who brutally murdered her grandmother, she teaches that through forgiveness there is peace after pain. Her recently released book Forgiveness: How to Let Go When it Still Hurts *became an Amazon number one bestseller overnight.*

She has been featured in many media platforms, such Women's Movement *radio show and the upcoming* 21 Answers To Emotional Freedom *on Women's Movement Television Network. The essence of her business, Find Your Courage, is transformational, intuitive, spiritual, inspirational, energy-boosting and action-oriented. Her services include private and group coaching, inspirational speaking, workshops and a number of programs that incorporate her Seven Keys of C.O.U.R.A.G.E., a seven-key acronym she uses to teach people how to live their best lives. Connect with Di at www.DiRiseborough. com.*

Lisa Diaz

The Transformative Power of Fear

Every morning, I have a ritual. I watch as my husband gets his flight suit on and laces up his boots. I look at the patches on his suit and I think about the stories they tell—how many deployments he's been on, where those deployments were, how many times he's landed on a carrier, which squadron he is attached to and, oftentimes, a patch to honor a fallen brother lost to an accident or a combat mission. Then we talk about what we expect from our day and who's taking which kid to piano, or to a baseball game. We exchange our schedules.

And then, every day, I make sure to ask one particular question—or, rather, two questions: "What time is your flight today; and which jet are you flying?"

You see, my husband's job is dangerous. He's a pilot for the Navy and flies the Hornet and the Super Hornet, both F/A-18s. He's just as handsome as you can imagine in his flight suit or his dress blues, and we're blessed in this life. But even at home, flying training exercises each day—maybe especially then—accidents happen.

I remember one day in particular, when I was going to do a pop-up boutique at an office in San Diego near the base. Just like every other morning, I had asked my husband my usual questions so I would know what and when he was flying. The women there were having fun, laughing, shopping. And then we heard an explosion, and the ground shook.

We rushed outside to see something less than a mile or so away, black smoke billowing up from the ground. We had no idea what it was until someone rushed into the office to say that a jet just went down. Immediately, they turned on the television news. Watching reports develop, I learned that it was, in fact, a Hornet, and that it was from that base my husband was attached to and from the squadron he is a part of.

That's why I ask my husband those questions. That crash happened at the time he was scheduled to fly, and it was his squadron. So I had to do what a good military spouse does—I had to wait. Stay off the phone to keep the line free in case I get a call and *wait*.

Pray that this time it was not him. And then pray it was not one of our friends. And then feel guilty about praying for favor when it sinks in that it IS someone we know, a brother or sister in our squadron.

I had to do what a good military spouse does—I had to wait.

Even though you want to call everyone, even though you want that comfort of a sympathetic voice on the other end of the line, you have to wait. Wait and pray. Because what if it was him? What if it was finally him this time? And what if it was not; who else could it be? What other spouse was going to get the news today? Everyone was asking themselves these questions, waiting at home as the news station confirmed the crash.

I was a lucky spouse that day. My husband called. He quickly said, "I can't talk. I am okay, and I love you and I don't know when I'll be home tonight." And that was enough.

Unfortunately, I have more stories like that—stories of waiting, stories of *fear*. My husband has, fortunately, been safe in his career so far, but, unfortunately, we have lost good friends who were amazing husbands and fathers and sons and brothers. So we know the fear, and I realized quickly that it can be paralyzing.

So I ask him every morning and I make a decision to do so. Every morning that I can, I ask him. If he's deployed, I can't, except for a phone call once a month—and that's a whole other fear—but whenever I can, I ask. "What time is your flight; and which jet are you flying?"

And then I say a prayer, for his protection and the protection of those he flies with, and I release that prayer to God. And then

---

I was angry that I was just sitting there.

---

my fear can be released and placed in the hands of someone much bigger and more capable than I to handle it.

God doesn't want us to live in fear. But fear is a part of life. We have to do our best prepare for it—in the military we do that by networking, making friends, creating support systems, even if we have to change them every few years when we're sent to another base. We reach out. We have to, because whom else can you fall back on when something might go wrong? Whom do you fall back on when the worst news comes?

We moved a lot, and so we couldn't settle. But neither could we decide to sit out and never make new friends—we had to do that all the time. And so we love fiercely and live boldly. We have to. But how much can we really prepare and how can we live like that with the fear weighing us down?

I remember my husband's first deployment to the Gulf. I was sitting in my office one day, and someone came running up— not knowing that this is not the best way to approach a military spouse—and said, "Did you hear?" as if she was excited. And then she told me two Hornets from my husband's carrier had crashed over Afghanistan.

I could have been paralyzed. But in that moment, I thought, *I'm done*. My husband was at risk, and I could only think, *I don't want to live small. And I don't want to sit here waiting for stuff to happen*. And that was transformative.

Fear is transformative. When you realize that you can use fear, let it remind you that life is precious and fragile and can be gone in an instant, then you can be free of its hold. It is not an obstacle—it's a motivator.

Sitting there in my office that day, I found my anger. I was angry that I was just sitting there. Because having a military spouse deployed to combat zones is not romantic—it can't just be waiting and pining. I had to use that energy that fear produces in a positive way to be what I wanted to be. And suddenly, I was less afraid.

And, thank God, my husband was not in either jet that went down that day, but that moment changed everything. I had always been afraid of some things. I was afraid to take risks for fear of

---

*Staring down the fear has
helped us together.*

---

failing. I was afraid to live boldly, to love with everything I have for fear of losing people I love.

But those were the things I needed to do. Those are the things we must do in order to live the best life possible, to be able to contribute to and have an impact on others. Choosing to stay limited because of fears is choosing to live small.

When you take control of your fear, stare it in the face and let it transform you and motivate you, you stop being afraid of failure. You start taking chances with your life, with business or with money or with reputation. You risk everything for a chance at success. And more importantly, you learn how to step out and live your life, all in.

In any relationship, you learn to be vulnerable, because rejection is just another fear. And so you say what you need to say and you stop being stingy with your words and your actions when you show your love for others. Living as a military couple with a dangerous job for my husband taught us to live with abandon and courage. Staring down the fear has helped us together. It's

---

We must risk and take chances to see what we're capable of.

---

helped us bond with our children, learn how to spend time with them and love them better. But it's also helped me for myself as well. For so many years I would have said no to anything too risky, but I learned that we must risk and take chances to see what we're capable of. Three years ago, I started my own business in my garage on a Navy base in California.

The business started out small, and grew and grew. It's purpose was to help others step out of comfort zones, to taste success and to discover they are capable of it. I particularly wanted to help military spouses, knowing at a very personal level the challenges they face, particularly when it comes to their careers. Now, although my business and career path evolved, I still get to help women see their potential, and live it.

When I started my business, I was committed to contribute financially to others in need, whether a military family in crisis or a wounded veteran returning home to a very different life. That commitment extended to helping children in other parts of the world who live in extreme poverty. Working with When I Grow Up, a nonprofit organization dedicated to giving children a different, hopeful future, we traveled to Nairobi, Kenya. It was an am amazing experience to be part of the life saving, transformational work When I Grow Up does in partnership with effective indigenous leaders. It was an opportunity to become part of something larger and more impactful than I could have ever imagined on my own.

That is what happens when we step out of fear: big things. Of course there is still fear and it can creep in when it comes to anything. Our responsibility is to see the fear and choose to move our feet in spite of it, knowing that action holds possibilities of greatness. I guarantee there will always be challenges, but you can face them head-on. You can push fear aside, step boldly forward and choose to make a difference for yourself and others.

Do the thing you've been putting off because you're afraid to fail.

A few years ago, I had to have surgery and had a cancer scare. I knew then that I had to have time for my children, plan a family trip, something—because of the fear that I might not have another chance. Thank God, I do. The fear isn't fun, but I know how to move with it to get me where I want to go and I'm definitely getting there.

And you can, too. You can let your fear open you up to a new, less scary world. I want to challenge you to have a ritual, like my ritual with my husband. I want you to challenge your fear every day, find a way to make sure you have control of it.

Take the limits of your fear, find them out and then use that to release yourself from your own limits. How can you do that? How can you make fear work for you? Personally, I make a list of what I'm grateful for and I pray. But you can do whatever you need to do to harness your fear and remind yourself that it doesn't control you. You control it.

If you're a military spouse, you might know all too well the disquieting sense of anxiety that comes from loving someone who puts his or her life on the line every day. Or you may know fear for other reasons—you've embarked on a new venture, or you're waiting for test results, or perhaps you're living with the fear born of regret, of ticking clocks, the fear that wakes you up in the middle of the night with the thought, "What if it's too late to follow my dreams?"

It's time to stop playing small. As often as we say it, you'd think we'd get the message: Life is short. Life is also unpredictable. You never know when you're going to get a call that could change your life. So step out. Do the thing you've been putting off because you're afraid to fail.

Use your fear to your advantage. After all, one sure way to know that your life is about to become amazing is the ever-present feeling of fear. If you didn't care so much, or want it so badly, you wouldn't be afraid at all.

Lisa Diaz is a mother of three and a military spouse. She is known for inspiring people to greater achievement with her enthusiasm, passion and insights, through conference trainings for many social selling companies as well as keynote talks. As a result of her years of experience in direct sales in founding and serving as CEO of Homecoming Trunk Shows, Lisa has acquired a broad base of knowledge that can make a significant difference for distributors, leaders and corporate executives. She now uses that experience as director of sales for All'asta. If you have been inspired by this chapter, Lisa asks that you visit www. WhenIGrowUp-Global.com to learn how you can get involved with their efforts to help poor and orphaned children grow up to pursue their dreams. She serves as head of business partner development for When I Grow Up.

Julie Stephens

Already Enough

I was in the ballroom at a conference when I had my realization. I can't remember anything else. I only remember being in that ballroom, a light bulb going on in my head. I was forty-six years old, and it was only then that I had the spiritual and physical maturity to receive the knowledge that I was about to receive. And the light bulb was lit by that knowledge. It was a knowledge I'd struggled all my life to realize.

I realized that I am perfect as I am. I am already enough. I am enough to realize my potential and serve my purpose in life. Everyone is. Even you.

It took a long time to come to this conclusion, however. It took overcoming substantial obstacles. To realize that we are enough, we have to shed the weight we carry around. It is like a backpack, filled and weighty with the perceptions, words and opinions of others that we choose to carry. We don't need to carry around that backpack; it belongs to the people whose perceptions are inside it. Only when we drop this weight, hand it back to the person or persons who gave it to us, are we free and capable of seeing our purpose to serve in our perfection.

My backpack was filled when I was young. I'll be honest, I was not a cute kid. I had bad haircuts, buck teeth and wore glasses. It was hard for everyone in my life to look past that. I was made fun of at school on a daily basis and can only remember having one true friend. My mother, going through a divorce, decided to take us to a counselor to make sure we did not think the divorce had anything to do with us and to help us cope. The only thing I remember about this visit is the counselor looked at me and said, "You do realize you are the ugly duckling of the family, don't you?"

I already felt that way. My sister was beautiful, blonde-haired and blue-eyed, while I was nothing of the sort. When I was younger, my mother kept my hair cut short, but I remember my sister's hair growing long and pretty. I saw myself in the mirror every day; I knew I was an ugly duckling. When this perception came from a person in authority, it became my truth, and it weighed me down in many ways for most of my life.

I'll be honest, I was not a cute kid.

In high school I had a small circle of friends. I didn't reach out to find new friends. Although I had braces in middle school to correct the buck teeth, and refused to wear my glasses, I still felt ugly. I didn't date boys from my school to avoid being the subject of gossip, because I knew the cruel things people could say. I could not emotionally handle any more baggage. I made myself a people-pleaser, because I thought that was all I had to offer. When I grew to adulthood I took additional steps to improve my own image and grow into the skin I'm in. I stopped caring what everyone else said. But for most of my youth, I looked in the mirror and saw the ugly duckling I was told I was.

I faced upheaval at home as well. When I look back, I see that my parents made mistakes. Back then, I only saw my "truth." I was a physically strong girl, constantly participating in sports. My sister was thinner and not as physically strong, and my parents used to ration my ability to fight back. My father's rule was my sister could hit me three times before I could hit back, for instance. My sister and I were very different people, not close as sisters and inclined to fight, so we disagreed often.

One day, as we shared clothes, my sister denied me a skirt that belonged to her, which I wanted to wear to work. We exchanged hits, and my thinner, prettier sister got a black eye. When my father saw it, he threw me out of the house immediately. I was told I could come back home once my sister graduated and moved out. I didn't understand. *Why did my sister get to stay? Why was I the one who had to leave? Wasn't I good enough to*

Raising my sons was a life-saving experience.

---

stay? We both fought!

The questions only continued as I was sent to my mother's house, where I was unable to pass at school. The message I received was: I wasn't good enough for that school, not advanced enough, and I would not graduate if I continued there.

To save my education, I was put in foster care and from there I could continue at my old school. I spent over six months with a foster family. I spent it in isolation, hiding my situation from everyone I knew, with the exception of my best friend at the time. The last thing they needed to know is that I was not even good enough for my own family. I felt discarded even with a warm place to lay my head. I was waiting for my sister to graduate and move out so I could go "home."

Why was I going through this? What was wrong with me that wasn't wrong with my sister, who was allowed to pack up all my things so my father could throw me away? The questions continued, even when I was allowed back to my father's house after her graduation, and I stayed there until I graduated myself. I left one month later to attend college in another town.

It was only a few years later that I faced a turning point. I never wanted to be a mother, but God saw fit to give me two amazing sons. I found myself a young mother and suddenly I had the unconditional love my family did not show me as a child. I could teach and guide my boys; I could lead them to good lives. I could teach them their worth. That allowed me to be myself in a way I had not before, and I was determined that my boys would not grow up the way I had. I would mess up; I would struggle, but they would *always* know how perfect they are. I only had one chance at getting this done right; there was no way I wasn't going to give it my all.

My boys are grown, and I did such a good job that sometimes they need to be reminded of their humility. I realized I had to do just as good a job with myself. Raising my sons was a life-saving experience, because they taught me self worth—they

I am already enough to serve my purpose.

showed me through their perception that I am worthy. Thanks to them, I've finally come to the realization that I am perfect as I am, as well, and I always have been. Even as an "ugly" child, I was who I needed to be.

Through this, I became that forty-six-year-old woman, sitting in her hotel room later that day at the conference, the past lit up by the revelations of the present. If I had turned my head and looked into the mirror then, who knows what I might have seen. I could see so clearly then how my burdens had held me back, and how I had grown and overcome despite them. I saw how I could shed them completely and move on to fulfill my purpose, my ministry, my service. I could see what I had to offer the world, now that the road behind me and ahead of me had opened up. Perhaps I could have seen all of this in the mirror, staring back at me reflected in the glass. I was full with the welcome weight of my realizations.

I am already enough to serve my purpose. Knowing this, realizing this, I have become even more successful than I was. I quit my forty-hour-a-week job to start my own corporation. Today I am the builder of multiple corporations that I am growing and will one day sell. I gave up steady work and a

---

Only you can define the limits in your life.

---

steady paycheck to do this, and I would never have risked that before my realization. Now, when I look in the mirror, I see endless possibility. I want to take this possibility, take the risks I know I can take now, and make it an opportunity to share this message.

In life, we have all been told something negative about ourselves. Someone will not like our looks, our attitudes, our abilities. And we've hung onto these words from others and created a "truth" from them for ourselves. But the real truth is that we decided to carry this message with us as if we were carrying that backpack. It hindered us; it strengthened the little voices of doubt in our heads. It caused confusion, self-doubt and lack of action. We don't have to keep carrying it along. We can identify that part of the voices in our heads and return it to where it came from. Don't let anyone define you or your abilities!

Only you can define the limits in your life. Earlier this year, I heard on the news a story of a very popular singer-songwriter. She has always been a huge success and a huge talent, already considered a celebrity. The news was reporting that she'd gone to rehab for an eating disorder, allegedly caused by her manager. She was told over and over again that she wasn't perfect, and he would make comments about her weight in a derogatory way. Her manager gave her the perception that she needed to lose weight, and she carried that perception all the way to rehab with an eating disorder. She was kept from her absolute potential by someone else's "truth." And now that she's emerged from it, spoken about it and realized that she doesn't have to carry that with her, she is facing her full potential. I hope she has now come to the same realization I have. Those words were someone else's opinion of her.

It made me wonder, how many celebrities face these same struggles? How many everyday, average people as well? How many throw away their potential because they believe themselves unworthy and listen only to what others think about them? How many let this stifle them so they can't even see their dreams? How many are carrying around their full backpack, weighed down and weary? The answer is that in every country, every state, every person, we all face this in our lives. We all share this experience and we can all be kinder to others, knowing this. I believed my message had to be heard.

I once believed I wasn't created for success. I got by, because that's what I was supposed to do. I met the low expectations placed on me and didn't aspire to anything higher. I settled, keeping the words said about me and to me in the forefront of my mind, letting them guide me. I held myself back from success, from fulfillment, from even thinking about dreaming of a bigger life. The bottom line was, I was breathing, but I wasn't living.

After my "light bulb" moment, I stepped out in faith and got out of my own way. I finally realized, "I'm no different than anyone else. Successful people don't have anything I don't have." Once I decided I was just as capable and deserving of an amazing life, I found the toxic root in my life and pulled it out. No longer would I hold on to the negative beliefs instilled in me as a child. I would not allow my mind to focus on those thoughts for a minute longer.

We are all created differently and perfectly for the purpose we are meant to serve. We are like puzzle pieces; there are endless colors and shapes and sizes, and all of them are needed to complete the puzzle, to make the picture complete. I dare you to find another puzzle piece that looks just like yours. You have to know that you are made exactly as you are for a reason. You are enough to fit into the world where you were meant to fit. *You were created like you on purpose!* Once you realize this, you can identify your purpose, shed the imperfect "truth" that you've been carrying around and achieve your goals, to where a perfect world opens before you. You will begin to see things differently, dream bigger, search deeper and succeed higher. All in the name of your perfection, your service to this world and your new mindset. Keep breathing and start living!

Julie Stephens is a transformational speaker and coach, and her business, Transforming the Tribes, focuses on supporting those who have ever believed they weren't enough, whether professionally, personally or otherwise. She helps her clients overcome the feelings that hold them back from creating themselves in their innate perfection and greatness.

Currently holding a real estate broker's license in multiple states and founder of multiple companies, Julie is one of two percent of women entrepreneurs in the United States who generate more than one million dollars in annual revenue. Connect with Julie at www. TransformingTheTribes.com.

Susan Staples

Just Fly!

There is no better seat on a plane than in the cockpit. As a commercial airline pilot, I saw the most beautiful cloud formations, sunsets, sunrises and starry nights—breathtaking displays of nature's wonder most people on this planet will never have a chance to see in their lifetimes. I have so much gratitude for these moments.

It was an honor to work with some of the most talented people on the planet as crew members. It is my long-held belief that the Captain may have the final decision, but those critical empowering choices come from hours of experience and the ability to listen to their crew. For me, knowing my decisions determined if we would make it to our destination safely and on time, connecting people to important business meetings, loving families and to long awaited vacations, gave me a daily dose of fulfillment. To leave all worldly problems on the ground and experience the freedom of flight was extraordinary.

One day, just before Christmas, I parked the brakes with the intention of having the holidays off so that I could have hand surgery for a nodule that had developed on my left hand while using the tiller wheel to steer the airplane on the ground. I had no idea that would be my last flight as Captain for American Airlines.

Within a couple of days, I was in the emergency room with severe stomach pains. I was diagnosed with gall bladder disease and was immediately grounded. After surgery, my body was in full rebellion mode; I worked through every diet imaginable, but nothing seemed to work. I was no longer able to digest normally.

The following year, while driving home from the bank, I was sitting at a red light when an SUV rear-ended me at a high rate of speed. The driver never saw me; he was on his cell phone. My neck jerked against the headrest and I immediately felt woozy.

From that moment on, my life began to unravel. It started with a whiplash diagnosis. Then, one of the chiropractors I saw for treatment triggered a neurological response in my body that sent me back to the emergency room. While snapping my back, he did something wrong that caused my vertebra to pop quickly one at a time all way up to the back of my neck. It felt as though the muscle along my spine was tearing. When it reached my neck, I suddenly felt as though there was an explosion of "funnybone" tingles around my skull, and the same wooziness returned. Later, my heart began to race, my right leg became numb, I was dizzy

---

From that moment on, my
life began to unravel.

---

and my head felt as if it was engulfed in the vibration of a tuning fork. I felt electrocuted as heat was coming dramatically out of the top of my head.

Four months, more than thirty ER visits, three hospital stays, four top neurologists and one cardiologist later, I still had no clear diagnosis. Bedridden and heavily medicated, it was determined I was not a surgical candidate. *What am I going to do?* I wondered. I was newly remarried, mom to a young teen and a professional woman just lying there listless in bed with no real prognosis. *What if I'm never able to walk alone again, or sit up on my own?*

What if I can't be there for my daughter? What if I become a burden to my husband? How would I pay my bills? I was so upset, so full of fear, judgment and blame. I was living with the mindset of a being a victim, drowning in doubt, terrified that I would never fly again. *What will I do if can't be a pilot? It was always my dream... now what?*

I saw my husband crumbling in his own inability to handle the stress of the situation. He became his own worst enemy and was not capable of staying as my caretaker. The stress that my health challenges placed on my family was more than it could sustain. My husband and I separated, and we began bleeding financially as we waited for insurances to kick in, spending money for help

---

**I was living with the mindset
of being a victim.**

---

to take care of me... and then to support separate places to live.

The neurologists, all with different specialties, were so confused. Tests came back inconclusive, or in conflict with each other. I was a "medical mystery." I was very frustrated because I wanted them to make me well.

"What's wrong with me," I asked out loud. "Why can't they fix me?" I started to doubt myself, and God, and the process—everything there was to question, I questioned. It seemed as though I was piloting an airplane that was out of control, about to crash into the side of a mountain, certain that I wouldn't survive.

Then I remembered what I would do if I actually were flying a plane that was in a crisis situation. I would use all of the resources available to me—my crew, the ground personnel, my training and experience—to make new decisions to stabilize the emergency.

As a pilot, I couldn't look at a potential outcome for a crisis and just let it happen. So why wasn't I willing to do that for my self? It was time to take responsibility for my own healing.

So, when one of my health practitioners asked me if I would be willing to "think outside the box," I smiled. I was familiar with that in aviation. We called it "Declaring an Emergency." Once the pilot states these very clear words to air traffic controllers, all of the normal operating procedures are no longer required. Declaring an emergency opens the door to creative lines of thinking about whatever could possibly get the plane on the ground safely.

He said, "I know someone who is uniquely qualified to understand what truly happened during the adjustment. He is a chiropractor, but he is also a fourteenth generation doctor of Oriental medicine, with an orthopedic specialty."

I agreed to see the new doctor and, after my initial evaluation, I found hope for the first time in my medical crisis. He said, "I can help you heal." He told me he could get me back to a somewhat normal lifestyle, with one exception—he wasn't sure if I could return to the cockpit again.

From my new doctor I learned how to come into acceptance for my situation. This was a valuable step in my recovery. I was no longer willing to live with the misidentification of being a victim. Instead, with every appointment I was empowering myself, using all of my resources to get the plane that was my body to safety.

Declaring an emergency opens the
door to creative lines of thinking.

I learned that once I accepted my health situation, I was able to begin letting go of what was holding me back from achieving any recovery. Over time, I was able to learn the process of healing. Even though the traditional doctors were full of compassion, they could not do what I needed to do for myself. I shifted my attitude and opened my heart.

My doctor taught me how to partner with him to give my body the "best odds to heal." I educated myself on every aspect of my body and I came to understand that food is a cornerstone of healing. Food triggers physical responses, but it also triggers emotions, and can be connected to how we feel about ourselves, our memories, how we show up in the world. I discovered what works for my body—where I was at the time, where I wanted to be and how making the right dietary choices for me could help me get there.

Within seven months, I was no longer on medication and I was able to do some limited driving. I experienced a lot of pain without the medications, but found it was worth it, because it afforded me the opportunity to fully experience the changes in my body. It also allowed my treatment plan to be more effective.

The most profound change occurred when I learned to forgive. I forgave the man on his cell phone who placed his engine in my trunk. I forgave the doctor who snapped my back wrong. I forgave

---

*I educated myself on every
aspect of my body.*

---

my ex-husband for his inability to see me through my healing process.

I forgave anything and everything I could and each time I forgave something or someone, my body responded favorably. My thoughts became more positive and, for the first time in years, I had hope for my future.

My life is completely different now. I have challenging days, but I continue to receive treatment and have learned to manage the internal tremors and other issues without medication. Due to a final diagnosis, I have not returned to flying. I have permanent damage to my right eye, a brain injury and neuropathy from an over-stimulated sympathetic nervous system. At first, the diagnosis seemed like a loss. From the time I was very young, I yearned to be in the sky and see the world. Fortunately, by the time I realized my aviation career was well and truly over, I had had a lot of practice with acceptance!

I've discovered that my purpose on this planet is to heal, and that is an ongoing process that I've accepted as part of being alive. I am choosing to create a beautiful business of speaking, coaching and writing about what I've learned in order to be of service to others on their own health journey.

I know first hand that the body will heal if given the best opportunity to do so. I have learned a new respect for all health practitioners, both allopathic and alternative. Both have valuable information and healing opportunities to provide. I know that an integrative approach works best. And I know now that healing a person takes place from the inside out. I have learned that, while responsibility is multi faceted, it has three distinct steps.

The first step is "Choice." This means to actively review and see what is working and what is not in your circumstances. This includes a willingness to look at both the inner choices and the

---

Healing a person takes place
from the inside out.

---

outer choices you are currently making and explore new ones.

The second step is to own it! Own your circumstances despite your own personal upset. Dr.'s Ron and Mary Hulnick say, "How you relate to your self as you're going through the issue IS the issue." It is about owning your circumstances and standing in the truth of where you are and who you are. This simply means: Stop blaming others.

The third step is to make new self-honoring choices that will support you and create what you need and want. For example, consider creating self-care rituals that nurture you as a whole being. By doing this, you can release any feelings of self-victimization and move forward very quickly.

I still feel that exhiliration I used to feel when flying—I feel it when I'm with somebody who has had a breakthrough, knowing I helped them get to that place. It is such an honor to be of service!

What really makes my day is to see the looks on the faces of the people I have had the honor to serve; to see how they shift and grow and heal; to see, years later, how their lives have changed, so that they are happy and smiling and living to the fullest—that is better than flying a an airplane, as its flight eventually terminates, but a person is elevated and continues to fly. I fly now in the choices I'm making in my new life, how I show up for this day. I will make it to my destination—a simple, happy, healthy life.

Final wisdom: Don't wait until you are in a crisis to take care of yourself. You will never reach your destination in your professional or personal life if you stay parked at the gate! Just fly!

Disclaimer: The opinions expressed in this story do not represent the opinions of American Airlines or its subsidiaries.

Susan Staples is a women's empowerment and self-care expert who helps overwhelmed women running on empty take back control of their health, wellness, and energy so that they can do the work they love, have time for the people they adore and experience the vitality that they deserve. Certified in integrative nutrition and with a master's degree in spiritual psychology, Susan offers personal coaching and group programs that weave spiritual context into a holistic approach for long-term weight loss, stress reduction, personal development and creating the life you've always dreamed of.

Susan's background of more than thirty years as an accomplished pilot who achieved some of the highest honors for women in the aviation industry, along with decades of service as an advocate for women's issues in aviation, give her a unique perspective of the obstacles women face and the resources needed to overcome them. Her personal experience with several significant health crises, leaving her heavily medicated and unable to function in normal daily activities, ignited her passion for nutrition, weight and stress management, spiritual clarity and the power of a balanced life. Susan has created a step-by-step self-care program, "You Reimagined," where women learn radical strategies to succeed through doubt, fear and crisis, and continues to inspire women as an author, speaker and coach for achieving elevated wellbeing and creating the life they want. Connect with Susan at www.FoodTherapySolutions.com.

Debbie Evans

Focus on the Moment

As I opened the door to the first of our Christmas guests, I wondered what they would think. I worried about the lack of doors to bedrooms and bathrooms, the insulation showing around the back door, all the areas of the house in which our remodel had stalled. *Would they notice? Would they realize just how bad things are for us?*

I had done my best, wrapping the back door frame in lighted garland, putting glass balls into bowls with little lights, decorating two trees. The house was a-glitter with lights and gold and silver shining ornaments, cozied by the garlands and the red and green colors of Christmas.

"Oh, Debbie, how beautiful," my guests exclaimed. "Your house is just gorgeous—so Christmasy!"

I looked around me at my sparkling décor and I knew, by focusing on family and friends, making them comfortable and enjoying my time with them, I had created one of the best Christmases we'd ever had.

It was another example of how being present in the moment was putting me in alignment to receive the good things the Universe had in store for me. But being present in the moment was something I had only begun to learn, and the dark clouds over our family had just begun to lift.

In 2009, our business had its best year. With the 2010 Olympics coming, we had a lot of projects on the go. I was working on the Athletes Village Project and the office of the 2010 executives. In six months we made close to half a million dollars in profit, and things were good. I was being featured as one of the top interior designers in Western Canada in a design book by Panache publishing. We were renovating our home. I had leased a brand new Mercedes and the money was a-flowing!

In February of 2010, things started to slow, then became progressively worse; we didn't get a single call in eight months. We had been immune from the economic downturn because of the Olympics, but once they were over, it was as though someone turned the tap off all of a sudden. The construction industry died, and many business struggled, including mine.

I thought I could get us through this, and things would pick up, so I rode the wave.

Only parts of each bathroom worked,
so we had to shower downstairs.

Our home renovation went on hold in 2010, because we had to put all of our money into the business to keep it going. Only parts of each bathroom worked, so we had to shower downstairs. The exterior deck had no railings. We had two functioning electrical outlets in the main rooms of the house with dozens of plugs in each socket.

For the next year or so, I took on projects that paid up front, just because I needed the cash, but I was working long hours for very little profit. I remember feeling so alone and scared to death and I often wanted to just give up and die. Night after night, I worked on my laptop in the dark thinking, *If I just keep working, marketing and advertising I can turn things around.*

I was desperately trying to find answers on how to deal with debt, researching bankruptcy, looking into consumer proposals, speaking with lawyers. I tried to figure out ways to sell things and attract clients, at the same time feeling guilty because I could not immediately pay my debts and terrified that I would let people down. Calls from collection agencies caused me so much anxiety it was hard to function day to day. I wondered, *How did we go from making half a million dollars in profit a year to this?* I felt like such a failure for getting into this position.

I often wanted to just give up and die.

When the anxiety was the highest and I could hardly breathe anymore, I would go down to talk to my husband at 3:30 a.m., and ask him to tell me something positive to keep me motivated to go on. He would sit frozen with a blank stare and say nothing. He didn't have the answers; he didn't know how we could fix things. I soon realized neither one of us could handle the pressure or uncertainty of what we were facing.

We might lose everything we had worked for.

I would go to bed frozen in fear and sleep only a few hours, then awake, realizing I didn't have a choice and had to keep going for the sake of my family. Chris stayed home with the kids for a year, while I moved to West Vancouver to try to get the business going again.

I was often resentful and filled with anger and wondered why I was responsible for our financial future. Putting the blame on my husband, I even consulted a lawyer about a divorce or separation. It's easy to blame those closest to us when money issues cloud our judgement during hard times, since we are so angry and scared. After a lot of soul searching, I realized I had lost sight of what was really important to my husband and me; my marriage was not the problem and a divorce was not in the best interest of our family.

In the summer of 2012, I had to sell a lot of our personal items, including the sauna that I loved, to get cash for groceries and daily living expenses. It was very hard to let go of the things I loved. I soon realized that these material items really meant nothing to me. It was a real awakening and quite freeing to release myself from the attachment to these material items, and I began to realize they did not have any affect on my happiness. I began to meditate and listen to motivational speakers: Eckart

If you just focus on the present moment,
you can pretty much accomplish anything.

Tolle, Byron Katie and others. This lifted me into a higher awareness and new level of thinking, and my head cleared.

I realized that it was actually in our best interest for Chris to be a stay-at-home dad for a while. He was able to be with the kids, so schedules were not interrupted. I was also trying to restructure the business so that Chris could do more of what he liked when he returned to work: project management. I was determined to learn from the mistakes we made in the past and build a more profitable business that we could both enjoy again, but I knew this would not happen overnight. I heard once that, if you learn from every mistake you make, you are not failing, you are learning to win.

Through my meditations, I've learned that living in the present is the most important thing you can do, and it's the only thing you should do.

I've found that life happens—accidents, illnesses, financial setbacks, business problems. We have to really try to keep out the chaos and the clutter and the noise and stay focused on each day. If you just focus on the present moment, you can pretty much accomplish anything. It erases all that noise and the chaos. When you get caught up in the clutter, you can't think straight enough to allow yourself a way out.

Now, instead of getting in a panic or having anxiety attacks or worrying about life the way I used to, I get myself centered and balanced. What has surprised me is that, once I lived in the present moment, the Universe seemed to conspire to send me what I need. I receive the answer to a problem or question when I put it out there. I have often thought that I need something right now to resolve a personal or business issue or need; I would receive a call from someone who could help me with a solution that would take care of what I needed—right out of the blue.

Every time I stepped away from the chaos and got myself centered, things worked out. Every time.

I used to think, *If I work all day and night and keep working and working seven days a week, things will be better.*

And then one of my business coaches said, "Take a weekend off."

"I can't do that, my whole world's crashing."

"Take the weekend off. Just do it. Take two days off and just

---

Before I go to bed I meditate and thank
the universe for everything I have.

---

totally remove yourself, get rid of your cell phone, everything."

I took the two days off and, all of a sudden, I had a whole new perspective on things. I made a plan of action and focused on what I wanted for my family. I thought I couldn't afford the luxury of time off when times were at their worst and worked continuously with little or no sleep, focusing on solutions. When you take the time to be present in the moment, all of a sudden the answers will come to you.

Before I go to bed, I meditate and thank the Universe for everything I have. Try it. At the end of your day, think about all of the wonderful and supportive people in your life. Give thanks for the things you do have. This ritual will program your sleep in a positive way. When you wake up, set your intentions for the day and think about what you want. Leave yesterday behind. And, most importantly, love yourself. When you start and end each day in a positive way, it's amazing how you begin to align yourself in the right direction and things will start to flow to you.

When times are challenging, remember to embrace these moments and understand that in every challenge there is an opportunity to learn. Though it was difficult to go through at

---

There's always a message, a
lesson, in every challenge.

---

the time, I'm thankful for what happened to us, because it has changed our perspective on life. I was complacent, living in a bit of a fog, and now I'm so much more aware and in tune with myself, my business and what is truly important to me. I embrace all feelings. And when I am present in the moment and I ask for things, I get them. It's as though I've connected with the Universe.

I've achieved my goal of rebuilding my business. Many people set goals because they learned they should from a book or a coach, but don't believe in those goals—they're just words on paper. When you focus on the present moment and believe in your goals, they happen.

To believe you can attain your goals, you need to set aside the negative self-talk. I had to learn to love myself again and stop beating myself up that the business was failing. *I'm a failure. I'm not a good mother. I have to leave my family.* As soon as I got over that negative self-talk and started to love myself and to show others even more love, then, all of a sudden, when I set goals, they were real goals that I knew were attainable to create the success I so deserve.

I now live a more stress-free focused life and I know I will be taken care of. I am closer than ever to my family, and my identity is no longer centered around my career. I want my children to grow up knowing that together we can get through anything as a family. Challenges in our lives mold us and prepare us for bigger and better things and I am stronger than ever. I am ready to embrace the next chapters in my life.

Debbie Evans, RID, is the owner of Debbie Evans Interior Design. Through her work, Debbie collaborates with clients to provide spaces of comfort and beauty without sacrificing functionality. During her over twenty-two years in the design business, Debbie's work has garnered nine Georgie Awards and two National Sam Awards through the Home Builders Association. She was featured as one of Western Canada's top interior designers in the book, Spectacular Homes of Western Canada, *and can also be seen in the book,* Perspectives On Design, Western Canada, *which was published in 2012. Debbie graduated with her four-year advanced diploma in interior design from Algonquin College, Ottawa, Ontario. Connect with Debbie at www.DebbieEvans.ca.*

Nancy Greene, Esq.

Failure Is Not the End

I t had been two months. Finally, I was about to get what I wanted: a meeting with the managing partner of the law firm for which I worked. I'd been negotiating becoming an equity partner, but I had decided, finally, to step up and ask for what I wanted. It was time for me to open my own practice, but keep it affiliated with this firm. I wanted the support of affiliation, the ability to work with a team, even while I had my own physical practice closer to home than the two-hour commute into Washington, D.C.

Now, at last, I could ask for what I wanted. What I *needed*.

Things didn't go smoothly. He scheduled a client appointment for me during our meeting time. I assumed we'd discuss my relationship with the firm afterward. Wrong.

He stopped by my office and told me he was late for a hair appointment. Maybe next week. Twenty minutes later, I went to the "bull pen" (the open office space for the junior lawyers and staff) to say "goodnight" to anyone still there. The "late" managing partner was leaning against the door jamb of an interior office and talking to the other partner. When he saw me, the managing partner jumped as if he was a startled rabbit—the White Rabbit, specifically, from *Alice in Wonderland*. "I'm late!" he said, scurrying around me. "I'm late for my hair appointment."

My heart sank. He wasn't going to meet with me. Ever. No matter how hard I tried, no matter how long I waited, he would always have an excuse. To him, his *haircut* was more important than me, more important than all the hard work I put into the firm.

How on earth did I get here? I thought. *How did I get to be this person whose work and time was so undervalued, who* let *it be so?*

When did my doubter's voice gain this power over me? It could have been any time, but I remember one incident in high school. We had an assignment to write on local color, and the teacher was speaking about my scene. She remembered it as this awesome and vivid piece, but not who wrote it. So she asked, "Who wrote this?"

I put my hand up, but she just looked at me.

She said, very simply, "No, you didn't."

After that, I stopped writing for years. That voice inside of me said, "Even when I'm awesome, no one believes it." So I just didn't try.

That voice inside of me said, "Even when I'm awesome, no one believes it." So I just didn't try.

Everyone has a fundamental insecurity; that voice inside us that says, "I can't do this." The voice that says we will fail. That voice kept me from making the right choices for myself, all the way into my law career. I'd done what I was "supposed" to do with a law career. I graduated from law school and joined a firm. My ultimate career goal was to stay with this original firm. I would go from associate to non-equity partner to equity partner, one of the managing team. And I was close—I was a non-equity partner with an eye on a management position. I expected to buy out one partner's position when he wanted to take a less active role in the firm (the definition of "retiring" in law). But it wasn't meant to be.

My time at the firm was bumpy, to say the least. I was abused by the staff, and nothing was done by the managing partner. When I said I wanted to take a more active role in management he said I wasn't "capable" of doing so. What a slap in the face!

Every morning, I woke up and said, "Please don't make me go there today."

To my hubby's credit, he always had the same response: "Okay, quit. We'll make it work."

Despite his encouragement, I stayed. I didn't have faith that we would be okay financially. So, I got up every day and did a job I loved in a place I hated.

There are a lot of reasons to justify being unhappy.

When I took a family vacation at Christmas, I was taken off cases in retaliation for taking the vacation. It was the beginning of the end.

"Fine," I said. I was used to this, but I was finished with it as well. I handed in my notice at my first firm.

"Fine," I said, as they reduced my notice period without consulting me, without notice, just two days later. I was used to it. I went on spring break with my kids instead.

At my next firm, one male partner told a pregnant associate that a women's highest purpose was to have and raise children. How insulting, not just to the working mothers in the office, but to all working women. If he really believed that, what did he think of me, a working mom with two children? But, I stayed. In this economy, we're told to accept what security we can. We're told to be grateful we're not on the unemployment line. There are a lot of reasons to justify being unhappy.

After a shakeup at my second firm, I decided to join a new company. The new firm promised me a lot. But I did something every lawyer will tell you not to do—I didn't get it in writing. I should have, because the honeymoon didn't last long. Within six months, I was dubious of what I considered the firm's questionable practices and once again fighting to go in every morning, which wasn't helped by a commute of two hours each way.

I was making bad choice after bad choice because I didn't think there were many other options. Then I decided to do something I had never done before: I asked for help. I consulted with friends in the same field. I listened to my husband when he urged me to quit. I listened to myself. I trusted in my vision of both opening my own practice *and* giving this firm a chance to work with me. I set up the meeting. When it was postponed, I set up another. When the next meeting was cancelled, I tried again. The final brush off?

"I'm late for a hair appointment."

That was it. I went home and, by the next day, I had emailed in my resignation. Not the most professional method, but they would not meet with me; it was my only option.

Giving up the golden handcuffs is hard.

One of the things about being a lawyer is your clients teach you at least as much as you teach them. Over the years, as I advised many business owners, I realized a lot of them were making the same mistakes and that those errors prevented them from realizing their business and personal potential. Once I had a very wise client who told me: "I never pick a fight I'm not sure I can win, and when I find myself in a fight I can't win, I get out as soon as possible." It took me years to fully understand her, and when I did, she was gone and I couldn't thank her. Thank you, Samnae.

Giving up the golden handcuffs is hard. The fear of uncertainty, the fear of failure, keep us trapped, miserable. I had never dreamed of having a solo practice. I just wanted to have a solid, valued voice. It never happened. I had brought these men significant revenue for years. And I was letting them dictate my self-worth, when their valuation of me was less than that of a haircut. So any lingering guilt was gone, and within a week, I opened my own practice.

As a friend, James Artimus Owen, says, "If you really want to do something, no one can stop you, but if you really don't want to do something, no one can help you."

While failure is always an option, it isn't an ending unless you let it be. It's your choice if you let it be the end. Quitting wasn't the end for me. It was the beginning. I finally realized that doubt and

---

While failure is always an option, it isn't an ending unless you let it be. It's your choice if you let it be the end.

---

fear are a part of life, and they can overwhelm us. We have the ability to overcome that and succeed against the odds.

Opening my own firm was terrifying and wonderful. Finally I could set my own schedule, be more involved with my family, and I wouldn't have to drive two hours each way to get into work. I brought all my clients with me and I secured an office. It was a nice moment, when I got to go to the little marquee and put up a little stick that said *Nancy Greene, Esq.* I woke up without dread, without the certainty of being growled at, without the inevitability of guilt if I spent time away from the office. I am more productive now—I *can* do this, and I have been doing it for eighteen months now.

There are key steps to take if you want to overcome your fear and aim for your goals. Legally speaking, there are three steps. First, make sure your groundwork is done; have your agreements *in writing.* Next, know what you're getting into; know the laws and rules of what you'll be doing. Finally, document and protect yourself from litigation.

The non-legal advice might be more important, though. Don't let fear hold you back. And listen to yourself. Trust yourself. I knew long before I acted that I could succeed. I let my fundamental insecurity hold me back. But now that I've let it go, I'm happier than ever. And you can be, too. Failure is not the end. It's your beginning. What will you do next?

Nancy Greene, Esq., has been working with businesses for the last nineteen years, helping ensure that those businesses can weather owner disputes and legal challenges. A member of the National Association of Professional Women (NAPW) and a NAPW Woman of the Year 2012/2013, Nancy loves working with other women business owners and helping them avoid legal landmines while running a business in today's litigious society. Repeatedly introduced as "not your typical lawyer," Nancy demystifies legal "mumbo-jumbo." She's was a speaker at Darnyelle Jervey's Unleash Your Incredible Factor 2014 and will be a speaker at the upcoming No Glass Ceiling in October, 2014.

Nancy earned her Juris Doctor from Catholic University of America in 1995 and gained invaluable, wide-ranging legal experience in other firms prior to founding Greene Law Firm, PLLC in Fairfax, Virginia. Also admitted to practice in Maryland and Washington, D.C., she is a trial-proven litigator as well as a trusted adviser for businesses on matters of employment law, business bankruptcy and ongoing operations. Nancy is an active member of several bar associations and the American Bankruptcy Institute (ABI). Connect with Nancy at www.ndglaw.com.

Colleen Hurst

Bitter or Better

"You're looking for justice, Colleen. This is not a just world," my attorney said. Sitting across from him at my desk, I couldn't believe what I was hearing. After everything—after financial and health crises, after multiple separations, after years of trying to get someone to hear the truth, to get my ex-husband to face that truth and to move our family forward toward a new reality *in spite of* that truth, I was just supposed to give up?

"Stop fighting," he continued, imploring me to understand. "You are not going to get justice, financial or otherwise. He may be a doctor, but you'll never get any money. It's not going to happen under the circumstances."

How could I let go of what I knew was right? I had tried too hard to get my husband to acknowledge the challenges he faced and to honor his family obligations and get help. Now, after the divorce, I was fighting for the future—for my children, and for myself. I was standing up for what was right and I wasn't willing to back down.

Not long after that meeting, a psychiatrist gave me another reality check.

She said, "Go and grieve for your ex-husband as if he died, because you will never see him again, and he will never see your children again." I thought, *This is crazy! This is impossible! That's not going to happen.*

Fighting furiously for what I thought was right, *to make things right*, had caused me to become an angry, frustrated, fearful person. The anger and frustration consumed me; the fear made me anxious about the future. Sometimes, these feelings immobilized me. I was not getting the answers I so desperately needed, which left me feeling stressed and helpless. Despite the toll on my physical and mental well-being, I still allowed myself to get caught up in the drama brought about by my ex-husband. I was in a world of chaos, dealing with crises that, most days, seemed insurmountable. Yet, I stayed in the fight.

I was on an emotional rollercoaster and I simply was not willing to get off. I spent time with other women who were bitter about their divorces, women who were caught up in the drama of their own failed relationships and lack of support. All day long I heard nothing but negativity, which reinforced my stubbornness.

Early in my career I was the Executive Director of a crisis intervention center for victims of violent crime. My strengths

*"You are not going to get justice,
financial or otherwise."*

were making change, finding solutions, problem solving, doing it with speed, finding resources to respond to crisis and doing it without feeling all of the above emotions. My goal was to limit the intensity and duration of the crisis, to find a solution.

Yet years later, I was having the very opposite reactions to my crisis and, because of the fear, frustration and chaos, I wasn't making the best choices. I was trying hard to find solutions but I was fighting alone. We had been together since high school, and I thought we knew each other so well; that he would do anything for his family. Even though he gave up on us, I hadn't been willing to give up on him. Later, after the divorce, I certainly wasn't going to let him give up on our two beautiful children—Karis, a sweet little girl, and Michael, a wonderfully mischievous little boy. It was too late for all of us when I finally understood I was fighting a losing battle.

One night, not long after my "reality check" moments with my attorney and the psychiatrist, Karis came into my bedroom, where I was resting on my bed. It had been another day of feeling sad and overwhelmed, and she decided she would make me feel better by giving me a foot massage with her "magic" peppermint lotion. As she rubbed my feet she repeated over and over, "Everything is going to be okay, Mommy."

I was on an emotional rollercoaster and
I simply was not willing to get off.

Moments later, Michael came in and jumped on the bed. "What's for dinner?" he asked.

I looked at both of them and started crying. Then I laughed. Suddenly, I got it: My kids wanted to be happy; they didn't care about being right. At that moment I felt an overwhelming love for my children and a profound need to protect them. *You have to do something.* Support was off the table, and I had to find a way to take care of my kids.

I thought about what my dad would do, what he would say about the situation. He was my hero and he had passed away on Christmas day in the midst of all of this chaos. I thought about my grandparents, and about the struggles they had endured when they first immigrated to Canada. I watched them work very hard and under great difficulty to grow their businesses and provide for their families. I saw them handle life with courage, strength and conviction. In that moment, I saw the truth about how I had been conducting myself, and it wasn't pretty. *My dad would not be proud of me. My family wouldn't want me to be bitter. They would want me to go down the path of* better. *I've got to handle this differently.*

When I realized that my family's core values and approach to life were hardwired into me, that I could easily tap into that and learn to cope better, to fight better, to live better, the light went on. It was time to move through this anger, find better coping strategies and re-establish a sense of control over my own life. I understood what needed to be done and now I had to do it. It was clear that I was going to raise my children alone and try to make a living for all of us.

I went to my family and said, "Everything has to change."

Seeing the joy on my children's faces, remembering the legacy of my father and his parents, hearing the relief in my family's voices, was my turning point.

Slowly, I let go of my anger. I laughed more. I let go of the people who were caught up in their own drama and reconnected with my two best friends from childhood, Paulah and Suzanne. Though they lived three thousand miles away, they happily

---

You have control over the choices you make.

---

became my constant and trusted confidantes. They had achieved so much in their own lives—one became a federal judge and the other the vice president of a major bank in Canada—and yet they never doubted I too would succeed.

Paulah and Suzanne said, "Don't do bitter. Do better."

Most of us are stronger than we think. Sometimes fighting alone can and will make you stronger. If we can put distance from the crisis and gain a perspective that is healthy, we won't just survive, but we will thrive. We will make better and smarter choices. Retrospect is a wonderful thing, and the most valuable lesson in all of this, to me, is how we manage crisis and fear.

I learned and must say, I sometimes learned the hard way, it's not really about *what* we're given in life, it's about *how* we handle ourselves, how we conduct ourselves through crisis, fear and frustration.

You must surround yourself with positive and supportive people both in your personal life and in your business life, people who will inspire you and empower you, even if you find yourself fighting alone. When caught up in the drama and chaos of crisis, you must find the quiet, take care of yourself and ask for help. Stay away from the negative feelings and the negative people. There are too many obstacles in both your personal life and your business life to let negativity get in your way.

***It's not what life hands us, it's how
we handle what life hands us.***

Maintaining a positive attitude is critical to your success! As much as I fought to try to control the crisis, I learned you can really only have control over yourself, not anyone else. You have control over the choices you make. I learned the lessons in everything that happened to me. I learned the value of working hard.

Every obstacle is an opportunity for growth. I fought the wars, I faced the battles. Adversity was a great teacher for me. It sharpened my instincts. It gave me better coping mechanisms. It made me fearless.

After my divorce, my mother loaned me money to purchase a modest home, and I went out and got not one, but two jobs. For a short time, I worked three jobs. One of those jobs was working as a recruiter for a staffing agency. I loved that job—I had found what I was truly passionate about.

It wasn't long before I started my own staffing company. Since I come from a family of entrepreneurs, that just made sense to me. I thought, *I can do this better.*

My strategy was to start slowly, build credibility, build trust and, most importantly, work toward an impeccable reputation. We were well on our way when the economic crisis hit. Our community was devastated and we lost over fifty percent of our customer base. I once again was thrust into adversity and challenge. It seemed as if we were starting all over again, but by this time I learned I had to work harder to persevere when challenged. I was determined to not just survive, but to thrive. In the five years since, my business has grown more than three hundred percent.

It's not what life hands us, it's how we handle what life hands us. Don't flee, don't freeze; instead, fight, but don't get controlled by your emotions. Get off the emotional roller coaster. Life happens, stay busy, stay positive, find your peace and stay calm! All of that will help you make smart choices. Take the time to find the joy in your life. My joy was right in front of me all the time: my children's faces. That joy will get you through it.

Get clear in your own mind what matters to you the most and stay focused. Keep your voice!

What is adversity teaching you? Which way will you go? Bitter, or better?

Colleen Hurst is an entrepreneur, mother and mentor. She is President and owner of ProStaff Employment Solutions, a prosperous, full-service staffing agency providing workplace management solutions and services. Her business has grown by 385% in the last five years, and she attributes that growth to strong and solid business values along with a passion for the industry. Her passion stems from a strong desire to create opportunities for people. Colleen believes strongly in being a responsible corporate citizen, and her company contributes to many community organizations and charities.

Colleen derives courage from people who have faced great adversity, including her father and grandparents, who fled to Canada from a nation affected by war and poverty. Her biggest inspirations and her greatest achievements in life are her children—her daughter Karis, a social worker, and her son Michael, a police officer. They kept her focused and determined to be the best she could be. Together, they have achieved much. In 2010, Colleen was selected as one of Windsor's WHO's WHO, fifty local leaders whose personal stories and achievements inspire. In 2013, she was ranked number twenty-two in the fifteenth annual W100 ranking of Canada's top female entrepreneurs by PROFIT *magazine and* Chatelaine *magazine. In 2014, her company was selected as one of Canada's fastest growing companies by* PROFIT500 *and* Canadian Business *magazines. Connect with Colleen atwww.ProStaffWorks.ca.*

Marybeth Rosato

I Almost Fell for It

"College? You can't go to college, we can't afford it"

My parents' words made my stomach ache and my heart sink. For most of my eighteen years, I pictured the life I was going to have as an adult, away from the town where I grew up. I dreamed of doing exciting things, traveling and learning. But I couldn't see a way out.

Throughout my life, I was criticized many times for being a "dreamer," even by people who didn't know me well. This would always be accompanied by a shake of the head and that laugh that seemed to insinuate, "Wow, you must be naïve. People like 'us' don't get to do things like 'that.'" But I was born with an "I Love Lucy" mentality and was always thinking of a master plan. Fortunately, I didn't give up on myself or my dreams.

Every ounce of trying and every new discipline creates opportunities that are not always directly related to the task at hand. Many times we reap rewards in other areas of life.

I had an after-school job at the local Burger King and cleaned classrooms with my sister at our high school to work off our tuition. In the summer, I had a job telemarketing for Olan Mills photography and another lifeguarding. I would get off work, bum a ride to the gym, take the classes, use the machines, shower and be ready for school the next morning. The gym closed at ten p.m.; I was almost always the last to leave. This was a pattern; many successes came to me after I had been doing things without fanfare when I was alone.

Here's one example. After my job and before going to the gym, I would visit my high school friend who lived nearby. Her mom was always so nice and always seemed interested in what I was doing.

She couldn't believe I worked so hard and asked, "Do you plan on attending college?"

"We can't afford it, but I'd love to," I replied. "That's my dream."

The discipline I put into other things in life paid off in a different way. My friend's mom went to a local Penn State campus and picked up all of the paperwork, financial forms—everything I needed to apply to college. Then, she helped me fill them out. Not only did I get in, four years later I graduated with honors and a special scholarship award that is now given each year. She saw what I could be, not where I was, and helped me make it happen.

---

*I dreamed of doing exciting
things, traveling and learning.
But I couldn't see a way out.*

I'm not sure how this all works, but I can count on it every time. It's the "Winner's Walk:" the lifecycle you can count on every time you set a worthy goal or have a new dream. It begins with an inkling, an idea that just maybe you can create a life that is bigger than what you have and what others expect from you.

Next, and before you even decide to follow that hunch, you share your excitement with those closest to you. This is where about ninety-seven percent of people stop dead in their tracks and don't make it. When you set a worthy goal that is bigger than your current state in life and of those around you, get ready for the countdown. You can count the minutes until the naysayers draw near. You will always know them intimately; many times you will be related to them.

We are both excited and insecure when we start something new, so we look for confirmation from others, from outside of ourselves. Telling those closest to us seems like the safest place to start, but, very often, it's not. If your goal is to climb Mount Everest, and you share it with someone who has never been rock climbing, what will that person say? "Why on earth would you want to do that? Be careful! You could get hurt!"

It's the "Winner's Walk:" the lifecycle you can count on every time you set a worthy goal or have a new dream.

When we don't share the same vision as other people, they really cannot imagine what we can see. This is why every organized group in the world meets on a regular basis, whether it's sales groups, real estate agents or whatever. It's so important to surround yourself with those who have a like mindset. How many people have talked themselves out of their dream because they were not in good company?

It's difficult when people have little faith in you, or put you down, because it seems as though your idea is impossible. But pay attention! This is where it gets good and exciting—but only if you recognize this stage.

Change is almost always accompanied by noise. Let the noise of the naysayers serve as a sign that you have chosen something worthy. When all of those around you are putting it down, in most cases it's a sign that you have outgrown your current state in life. Remember, the Bible says that "all good will be attacked."

In the next stage, you resolve and decide. Your paradigm has now shifted. Something inside of you has changed; you can see your goal off in the distance and you know it's going to happen. When you decide, your energy shifts and you are more powerful. You walk and talk differently and carry yourself in a new way. Others pick up on your enthusiasm and you draw into your path what you need because you are thinking forward and focused. This is what is often referred to as "beginner's luck." There is no such thing, it's simple resolve mixed with newfound energy that is helping you attract what you need directly into your path.

When I first got into direct selling, people said, "You're giving up your business degree from Penn State to sell lipstick? Do you really think you can make this work? Do you know how many people fail at that sort of thing?"

Since I was painfully shy at speaking even with just a few people present, agreeing with the naysayers' comments would have been an easy way out. But I knew better. I had already achieved one impossible dream by graduating from college. Why not another?

After my training, it took three full months for me to host my first four-person party. When the party started, it was worse than I feared. Four words describe that experience: full-blown panic

---

Change is almost always
accompanied by noise.

---

attack. I was so far out of my element. I could think of really great things to say—after everyone left!

I would lock myself in my master bedroom closet with a script I had written on a note card to help me follow up with prospects and book future business. I dreaded it. I never looked at potential clients as friends, so I was never relaxed. I looked at them as someone to be afraid of, because I knew their reactions could make or break my fragile sense of self.

I started hiding a tape recorder in the corner during my parties, then I would stay up late after the guests left and painstakingly go over the recording. Listening to myself was like nails on a chalkboard. I would stop the tape and figure out how I could overcome objections before they came up, simply by adding the answers to the most frequently asked questions to my presentation. Little by little it started to work.

Next, I built my team. I had twenty face-to-face interviews, which each took an hour, before I sponsored my first team member. I was awful at recruiting. I kept getting rejected and then would ask for feedback. Most said it all "sounded complicated." I wanted to be up front so they wouldn't be disappointed down the road, but I was telling them way too many details. I starting working on that aspect of direct selling as well and by my second year in

When you decide, your energy shifts
and you are more powerful.

business I was the number two sponsor in the entire company. The very next year, I was the number one sponsor and built the number one team. I repeated these titles many times. For a time, I was even the lead on the DVD that came in every kit showing how to run the business. Me? Was the woman who had a panic attack at her first party now showing thousands the way?

Thank God I didn't fall for any negative comments or predictions from those closest to me, or my entire life would be different. Had I waited for their approval my entire life would have passed me by. It's not where we start, it's how far we come.

Several years later, my company asked me to become a corporate regional vice president. The doubters and naysayers were louder than ever before: "How are you going to travel and speak all over the country when being a great mother is your main priority." And, "Are you trading your family life?" And, "You are walking away from the team you have built." I heard it all, and I worked it all out.

Many times I would get to the airport at four-thirty a.m. for a six a.m. flight, speak for three hours, fly back and be home before my children walked in the door from school. My husband's company was closed every other Friday. He was home, so it was an opportunity to hit multiple cities. It was a great experience, and I grew in every way imaginable. At one point, I had seventeen states plus eastern Canada and more than thirteen thousand people on my team. And to think I almost fell for it and almost turned down the position! Where there is positive change, there will always be noise from naysayers. Count on it, every, single time.

Even if we can clearly see the destination, we cannot always see how our path is going to unfold. We have to be flexible as to which way the path winds so as not to get stuck and lose an opportunity. After our beginner's luck stage (remember, there is no such thing; we simply are drawing everything we need into our path because we are attracting it through our new-found energy and vision), we go through many ups and downs. At times, we lose our vision completely. We suffer criticism; we go way up and then way down a number of times; sometimes we lose hope.

Nothing we do is ever just about us.

Then, just as we are close to hitting our goal, we usually suffer a major setback. It's as if God is saying, "I know you deserve to reach this goal but I want to see if you really have faith enough to push through this last obstacle so that, when victory is yours, it will be that much sweeter."

This is when many turn back—just before their major breakthroughs. Do not fall for this! Continue engaging in massive action, beyond what you have done before. Yes, all the good emotions have abandoned you during this stage. This is your personal "dark night of the soul" I have heard it said that motion creates emotion, so you must stay in action during this stage. Everything you walked through will be worth it. You will have won.

Nothing we do is ever just about us. We cannot give up or give in because those who were our biggest critics are watching. Remember, they have lost their dreams, or given up on them, and when you accomplish *your* dreams, it gives them hope. There is no greater gift.

What is your rocking chair story going to look like? Will it be a place of regrets, thinking back on all the things you woulda, shoulda, could have done? I never picture a rocking chair in the traditional way. I visualize it as a place where I tell my great grandchildren my adventures, and the times I pushed through barriers. My "I Love Lucy" moments. A rocking chair is not just a place to move back and forth. To me, it's a place where I look back and tell stories of how I was rockin' life.

Marybeth Rosato is a dynamic and insightful sales and marketing professional, acknowledged for top sales and recruiting performance and success in motivating an audience, sales teams and sales leadership.

She has a twenty-five-year success story in the direct selling industry. In her first thirteen years in the industry, she "walked the walk." Year after year, Marybeth paved the way for others by achieving number one recruiter and leading the number one team in the nation. Chosen as a featured speaker at all company conventions during her time in the field, Marybeth has had one of the top-selling audio CD's year after year. After a successful sales career, Marybeth spent the second half of her career on the corporate side of direct selling as a regional Vice President. She directed and guided a sales force of more than thirteen thousand consultants who generated more than twenty-five million dollars in sales.

Marybeth wrote and hosted the talk show BC Connect, *where she interviewed guest TV celebrity and former Miss USA, Ali Landry. The talk show was filmed in front of a live audience of a thousand guests for the Confidence Forum for Women. Among other notable accomplishments, Marybeth launched the first international market in Malaysia and was handpicked to present at the European Summit for Tupperware Managing Country Directors in Paris.*

Marybeth is also a certified Direct Selling Women's Alliance coach.

As a speaker, she shared the stage with Darren Hardy, Publisher of SUCCESS Magazine, *and several other top speakers and direct selling corporate executives at the SUCCESS Symposium in Dallas. Marybeth has also been keynote speaker and presenter for women's clubs, high schools and colleges on the topics of leadership, personal development and making a difference for the future. She serves on the board of a leadership camp for youth. Connect with Marybeth at www.MBinspired.com.*

Joyce A. Brown

A Funny Thing Happened on the Way to Success!

You may recall the hilarious, long running, Tony award-winning, Broadway comedy, *A Funny Thing Happened on the Way to the Forum*. Well, a funny thing happened to me on the way to success. In the play, characters living in adjacent homes on an ancient street in Rome discover a case of mistaken identity.

Though I never lived in Rome, my identity, too, was truly mistaken… by me.

I grew up on a farm in central eastern Indiana, about as different from Rome as you could get. My father was a farmer, and my grandfather before him. So the dinner table conversation at our house was not about conventional business, but about the price of pigs or wheat for the week.

Don't get me wrong. I wouldn't want to diminish farming life, or take anything away from my father or any farmer. They work very hard running high-risk businesses. Cows have to be milked when they're ready to be milked, and the grain harvested when it's ready to be harvested, which means farmers work in any condition. Rain, shine, snow, sleet; if they're sick or healthy; if they're tired or fully of energy; if all is well and if times are tough.

However, growing up, I didn't see farming as a business. Instead, I romanticized the thought of corporations and entrepreneurs.

(Get me off the farm!) I viewed business people as sophisticated and well-educated and I was convinced that all of those men and women who worked in those big buildings I saw on television, and in movies must be really smart. I wanted to be one of them.

After stumbling through all of those ridiculous first jobs we all held while trying to find our way in the world (I'll keep some of mine to myself—you do the same—but my favorite was soda jerk), I landed in sales.

I loved it because in sales you have some autonomy, a responsibility for a given arena. I always looked at it as it though was my personal business, with the company that employed me acting as the bank. Obviously, if you don't pay the bank back, it shuts you down, so there was always plenty of motivation to keep moving!

I ultimately became successful in my industry. I sold services to Fortune 100 and Fortune 500 corporations at the "C" level and became well respected by my peers. I led the formation of professional groups within the industry, spoke at national conferences and contributed to the cultural growth of my

A funny thing happened to me
on the way to success.

company. During this time, I began to learn the critical role that culture plays in business.

I worked in corporate America as long as was necessary to support our family goals. Once that was accomplished, I said "I'm outta here," and left to follow my dreams of becoming an entrepreneur. I had loved business since I was a child and now I wanted to make a difference in the world working with the people who keep our world anchored—entrepreneurs. My last year as an employee, I made a mid-six figure income and left on my own terms, feeling accomplished and capable.

So there I was, self-educated, self-trained and successful. I figured, "Success means I understand how business works and I'm able to pull it off."

Not so fast. As is true for most entrepreneurs, I didn't start out with maximum capitalization. (You know, so much money you don't know where to spend it first!) In other words, I was working on a shoestring budget to get things going.

Had I known I was in in kindergarten? Absolutely not!

My first smart move was to hire a business coach. A very professional, attractive, caring, bulldog, leader, who helps me prioritize and learn and shares with me where and when to go to get more information.

However, several months into my new venture, I realized, "I'm not calling my coach a lot. I'm just working with our regularly scheduled meetings."

I took an honest look at my business and saw that many times, I was not getting things done in a timely manner. "You know why, Joyce?" I said to myself. "You're a kindergartener taking entrepreneurship 101."

Had I known I was in in kindergarten? Absolutely not! After all, I'd been in business for years. I walked the walk, talked the talk, overcame huge business obstacles, managed to work through business politics and trained several new bosses over the years, all without losing my job. How could I be at the level of a kindergartener when it came to running my own business?

Now, I feel just plain dumb some days. I have tools available to me that I don't know how to use, partly because I haven't had time to study them and partly because I just don't know how. I have schedules that I have set for myself that I can't keep up with and I haven't yet found a calendar system that works on all of my technology and serves my needs to share with others. Something so simple takes research and time to figure out. Everything has to be figured out! (Anybody else want to share?)

Do you know what kindergartener entrepreneurs do? I spend hours and hours researching things on the web. This is pretty challenging because I don't know what to ask for, let alone what to do with it after I get it. Here's a great example: In an effort to save time and money, I purchased software so that I could make eBook covers on my own. WHAT WAS I THINKING? I am not a graphic artist! I am used to calling the marketing department and explaining what I need.

At my former company, the excellent copywriters and graphics folks understood me and our business. In no time they would send me a proof to review for approval. Now I have to do everything they did on my own. Staring at the software instructions I said, "I have to do what with Photoshop now? I don't know what a jpeg is! Are you kidding me?"

I know my area of expertise well, but everything I need to build around it, to deliver it to the world, is new to me. I am now the receptionist, marketing department, branding department, sales

---

I felt inadequate for the job at hand.

---

department, public relations department, web designer, creator of all processes and procedures and the accounting department. Oh please! Oh, and I almost forgot: I am the Culture Czar, building the culture of our company. It is so important to be clear about and mindful of what we stand for in the marketplace and the way we interact with our customers.

The realization that I had to wear so many hats (when I wasn't even sure how to put some of them on!) brought me to complete breakdown. Breakdown with me looks like throwing my hands up in the air, slamming the desk drawer shut, crying for a while and quitting for the afternoon. Then, crying again while I work the next morning. I felt inadequate for the job at hand.

I wondered, *What is my identity now?* I thought a seasoned businessperson would know what to do. I thought I would know what to do. This is not my first rodeo. Where do I go from here?

Well, the first decision is: I'm not stopping, so that option is off the table.

After I realized I was a kindergartener, and came to terms with all of my entrepreneurial responsibilities, I was humbled. For the first time in a long time I thought, I don't know how to do this.

It was hard to admit, but within a few days I realized that being humbled is actually a great place to start. From this place, I quit trying to have all of the answers. I gave up on having to be good

---

Own your kindergartener status and shout it from the rooftops: "I don't know!"

---

at every aspect of my business. I even gave up having to learn everything I thought I needed to learn. And finally, I picked up the phone and asked for support.

These days, I'm honest with myself. I surround myself with powerful, smart, seasoned entrepreneurs who know the path to success. I connect with other business people through my personal network and the through the organizations I have joined in the past couple of years, such as eWomenNetwork. Sometimes I'm embarrassed to have to ask some of the questions I need answers to, and I'm especially embarrassed when I have to ask twice. My corporate, non-entrepreneurial brain often doesn't get it the first time! When I'm embarrassed, I remind myself: "Where do you think these successful entrepreneurs started out? In graduate school? They started out as kindergarteners too."

We have to be willing to accept that we don't know everything, and that there may be some aspects of our business that we never fully understand. Just because you're new to something doesn't mean you can't become a successful businessperson. Nothing and no one can keep you from your dreams, except you.

Own your kindergartener status and shout it from the rooftops: "I don't know!"

Other experienced entrepreneurs really do want to help and make a difference for you. Now, in addition to our regular meetings, I call my coach when I need her. I'm honest with her; I don't pretend to understand everything and I ask for help. She encourages me.

She says, "Becoming an entrepreneur is not as easy as it looks!" (No joke!)

She also says, "Everyone, regardless of where they start, goes through a similar growth process. They face the same feelings and challenges you've had." (Is she sure about that?) "They are basic to the task."

An amazing thing happens when you give yourself permission to not know. It sets you free.

With freedom comes the truth. Now I understand, the whole will be bigger than the sum of it's parts. This is not about me; this is my company. I was given this idea, but the whole universe awaits its impartment. I take a deep breath, restart my engine, and it feels fun again, creative, exciting and uplifting.

A friend recently told me that what we do as entrepreneurs is not really work and she is so right! It's a quest to serve. Strength comes from believing. So, from this point on, I re-create my journey.

And for those of you who are on this journey with me, I say, "Let's do this!"

Joyce A. Brown is founder and CEO of Sellng Your Style, a company dedicated to helping entrepreneurs increase their sales results. Joyce teaches her clients how to sell based on their own personalities and styles of relating to people. Her sales methods are especially effective for people who dread sales, people who are afraid of sales, and people who believe they cannot sell. After decades working in corporate America, selling corporate relocation services to Fortune 500 corporations such as AOL, Nissan, Time Warner and Gulfstream, Joyce retired to pursue her lifelong dream of becoming an entrepreneur. She is a certified relocation professional and a global marketing specialist; she co-founded HOA Management Directory. Connect with Joyce at www.SellingYourStyle.com.

Tara MacDonald

Directing the Movie of My Life

In November 2006, I sat on a plane, feeling as if my world had shattered. I was confused and frightened, and I spent the six-hour flight with tears of grief in my eyes, every mile bringing me closer to the unthinkable: the funeral of my dad. He'd died suddenly of a heart attack at age sixty-two, and I felt as if I not only lost my rock, but I lost myself.

My dad had been the only person I could always count on. In 2002, he had taken me in after a disastrous experience at a publishing job left me with no income, no financial independence and a lot of anxiety.

For the next four years, he'd given me safety and stability as I slowly rebuilt my life into what Dad wanted for me—working on a business degree he had chosen and paid for and preparing to take the reasonable, linear career path he planned for me. I had just recently moved away to work in Calgary. And now the most instrumental person in my life was gone.

The next few days were some of the darkest in my life. Surrounded by my dad's family, who barely knew me, I could hardly breathe under the weight of the devastating loss. I walked through the empty house before the funeral and all I had were desperate questions: "What am I gonna do without my father?

What is going to happen to me?" Little did I know that my dad's passing would become a catalyst that would let me find my own strength.

The funeral was where I truly understood just how alone I was. I was in the church, with my father's body in the casket, when a church friend started a conversation with me about how I needed to sell the house. He was a realtor, and up until that moment, I had considered him to be a respectable business professional. As I recoiled and withdrew my hand from his grasp, I looked around and realized no one would stand up for me now if I didn't do it myself. No one would protect and shield me as my father had.

The "old" me—the devoted daughter who did as she was told—would have listened to the whole spiel politely. Not this girl, though—not anymore. I told the realtor it was neither the time nor the place for his advice and asked him to leave. As I walked out of the church with my family after the service, I felt the wind on my face and I knew from that moment, I would be carving my own path. No more falling in line with anyone's expectations

---

I had to start making my own choices because there was no one to make them for me.

---

or living someone else's dream. I had to start making my own choices because there was no one to make them for me. The protective cocoon, as suffocating as it was safe, was gone.

I decided to move into the house I inherited from my father, which set a whole new slew of challenges before me. I didn't know where the oil tank was, or what to do with the propane fireplace, or how to manage a house built in the eighties. Even when I had lived with my father, I didn't have to worry about things like hiring someone to shovel the driveway in winter or taking care of the lawns. It was a lot to take in, but I was a fast learner. I went through seven different contractors, but I finally found an honest one to help me maintain the house. And I didn't stop there.

In December, I enrolled in film school. I had always dreamed of working in film production, but it took my dad's death for me to realize that I wanted to make this dream happen. It was not something I would have done if he was still around— he had disapproved of the idea, convinced I would end up as a starving artist. But I was now the commander of my own ship, and there was no one else to make these decisions for me. So without anyone's input or advice, and with no one backing me up financially, I just did it. I entered film school with the goal of starting a film production company.

I knew my goal from the very first day, and that made me immediately different.

When the classes started in January, I was full of elation, but also fear of heading into the unknown. This was different than being a business student, after all. At the same time, it felt really empowering to walk through that door and sit in those classes: I was giving myself permission to be who I was. Most of the other students were younger and they all wanted to do something with their lives, but most of them didn't know what it was yet. I knew my goal from the very first day, and that made me immediately different. The feeling of accomplishment it gave me made me believe that I could succeed.

Barely a month later, I registered my company. I named it Charlie Mac, after my Dad. The beginnings were not easy. I still wasn't sure I would be able to survive on my own, let alone run a business by myself. There is only so much you can learn in business school, and over the next few years I had to face many challenges that I didn't feel prepared for: audits and payroll errors, benefit programs and film sets where everything went wrong. What helped me most was what my dad had so often told me when I had a tough exam or a bad day: "Never, never give up." Whatever life brought my way, I held onto those words and made myself go on, no matter what. I was born out of the fire of 2006-2007.

By the time I decided to close the company in 2013, we had done it all: We had won awards and done corporate work, made TV commercials and *pro bono* music videos for starving artists. I had been able to contribute to the local economy and help people I hired get experience that they needed to further their careers. I had a wonderful team that was constantly getting better. The last year had been our most successful. But I wasn't satisfied.

I was working sixteen-to-eighteen hour days and that was taking a toll on me. Working with a CTI coach, I began to realize that what I was doing didn't fit my needs anymore. I wanted other things in my life—a family, a partner, more time for myself and my dogs. I needed to take care of my health, too—the older I was, the more I realized that our time on Earth is short, and if I didn't want to end up like my dad, I needed to take care of myself. The loss of my aunt to breast cancer at the end of 2012

*I was living my dream, but
dreams can change.*

only strengthened my conviction that it was time to move on.

I was living my dream, but dreams can change. People often believe that life is like a movie—a shining moment of realization, a life-changing decision, and everything is different; we can ride off into the sunset, toward our happy ending. But life doesn't work like that. It's a process. We reach one goal, learn one thing, and it builds a foundation for new plot developments and further character growth. It's a constant evolution. I needed to survive my dad's untimely death to learn to rely on myself and I needed the experience of managing the company by myself to gain confidence and realize I could do it. But the biggest challenge for me is a more personal one.

I have struggled with my weight since college and now I really want to focus on my health and wellbeing. As a plus-sized person, I know how hard it can be to step into the gym where everyone seems to be judging us, and how easy it is to injure ourselves if we try to do too much, too fast. In 2006, in my quest to find a beginner fitness program I could do at home, I discovered Beachbody. When I got an e-mail from my Beachbody coach in October 2012, saying that the company was coming to Canada and was looking for people who were interested in multilevel marketing, I knew that was it. "Yes. Yes, that's what I wanna do," I said.

> *I know what fear tastes like; I've been there,*
> *and if I could overcome it, so can you.*

Being a Beachbody coach fits my needs perfectly, allowing me to use my management skills to really help people and to work on getting myself healthy and fit at the same time. Most of my clients, men and women, are plus sized like me and seeing someone they can identify with helps them believe they are not alone in their struggle. They talk to me, knowing I understand their challenges, and together, we get things done.

But it's not just being plus sized that makes me perfectly suited for being a coach. I believe my whole life experience—the business degree, Charlie Mac, the struggle after my dad's passing—builds up to the role I play now. Two of the biggest barriers for plus-sized people who want to get fit are self confidence—or rather the lack thereof—and overcoming fear. They don't believe they can succeed, so they need someone to assure them they can. I still remember what it feels like to stand at the brink of a big challenge, not feeling remotely certain I can do it. I know what fear tastes like; I've been there, and if I could overcome it, so can you.

You too can keep going forward, always pushing on, and never, ever giving up. There are people around you who can help you and want to help you with whatever you're going through, whether it's your own fitness regime or another challenge that you or your life put before you. You can do it, but you have to keep going, because no one else will give it to you—you have to give it to yourself.

What's next for me?

Who knows! I recently discovered I love to write—I'm curious to see where this new plot twist in the movie that is my life leads me. One thing I know for sure: I feel more alive now than I ever did.

Tara MacDonald is a Coaches Training Institute (CTI) trainee, working on certification and leadership in 2015 for her coaching business, Tara MacDonald Fit Club. An Associate Member of International Coach Federation (ICF), she holds a BA in English literature and a BBA in marketing and management and is currently pursuing her dream of achieving her MBA. Previously an owner of an award-winning film production company, Tara currently hosts and organizes two nonprofits (Find Your Feet Walking Club and NS FIT 4 U) with the goal of making fitness approachable for anyone. Working for Beachbody as a direct seller allows her to fund these nonprofits and helps her reach her public through free workouts and Shake 'n' Shares. Connect with Tara at www.TaracMacdonald.com.

Florence Onochie

Love, Learn and Lead with Focus and Balance

I was rushing to pick up my children at daycare when the cramps began. *Oh, no,* I thought, *something is going on. Am I having a miscarriage?* I pulled off to the side of the road and tried to calm down. I had a successful career in banking and accounting, a happy marriage and two delightful children—I was pregnant with our third child. My work took me all around the state of Indiana. Often I'd be up and away by six in the morning. On some days I would have to leave my work early—and so not fulfilling my responsibility—to pick up my children before the daycare closed at six in the evening. On other days, I would have to pay an evening babysitter to pick up my children and care for them until I got home. I was also paying a housekeeper, because I could not keep up with the housework.

What am I doing with my life? I wondered. *Yes, I earn a lot of money, but it goes to pay other people to care for my children and my home—there's nothing left for me. Has my success brought me a lifestyle I really want?*

There by the side of the road, it became clear that my life had lost balance. My focus on my career had led to success, but that work had taken over my life. My time was not my own, and I certainly wasn't spending every minute of every day in a way that was responsible and purposeful for my family.

God had given me children, a blessing and a responsibility, and I was leaving it up to others to raise them. Something had to change.

I have five children in all; for ten years I was either pregnant or holding a baby. My pregnancies were difficult. I often needed a rest from work for the last months, and this held back my progress in my career. But even more important was the need to care for, nurture, guide and instruct my children. That was my primary responsibility, and that should be my primary focus.

I was living my dream, but dreams can change. My husband and I decided that it was time to quit my corporate job and start my own business. My children will stay at the daycare during my hours of work and I will have my own flexible schedule. As my children grew older, because I have my own flexible schedule, I was able to schedule time for their activities.

At first, it was difficult to find balance while building my business. Growth is slow, and the business required a lot of my time and energy. Still, I was able to schedule my business responsibilities around the needs of my family—it was worth it.

Has my success brought me a lifestyle I really want?

It did not take a long time; I started making more money as an entrepreneur than I was making as a career woman and with fewer hours spent working.

Keeping my focus on having a balanced life helped me to achieve it. Had I had a fractured focus, I might have ended up in a similar situation, having little time for my children. I made every decision with balance firmly in mind. For example, I knew what type of client I needed to keep the lifestyle I wanted.

By keeping my intention and goals clearly in sight, I was able to say, "This is what I want, and this is how I want to do it."

During this era, I discovered my strengths and started applying them in every role I played. I turned my ideas into actions, conditioned myself as an expert and began to be noticed for what I could do.

I was living my dream, but
dreams can change.

With my life in balance, I was able to open my heart and listen so I could find out what my clients wanted and lead them in the right way. I learned to do positive things to boost my energy so I could be more productive, to clear things out and simplify my life so that I could achieve better results in less time.

Now, I am building from my education and experience my journey as an author, speaker and coach. With my children grown, my focus is on reaching my unique potential and leaving a legacy. I started honoring my gifts and the message I had heard from family and friends for so long: "You have the power to shine light onto others."

One day, after finishing a lecture, one of the attendees followed me out of the room to ask me a question. It took a long time to answer, and the next speaker was about to take the stage. That's when I realized: "I can't take care of everybody one-on-one. I need to make sure they have a book so they can read it whenever they need it. If I am not there, my book will speak for me." I wrote many books, and they have been a great joy in my life.

I have taken a lot of risks over the years. Facing my fears and challenges is something I am proud of. There are disappointments in life, but over time I've come to know for sure that I can handle any circumstance that comes my way. Problems come and go, and life goes on. When you have balance between work and family, managing any problem is so much easier.

We all have the ability to reinvent ourselves and grow in a way that is compatible with our responsibilities. You can achieve what you are meant to do in life without sacrificing your well-being or the well-being of your family.

Anyone can do it with the proper focus. Decide what you want to do, and find a way to achieve it. If you don't have the skills, seek help. When you try to do everything on your own, you are living and working out of balance. Find people who specialize in an area you need help with and connect with them.

The number one key is to be passionate about what you're doing. If you have passion, you will be happy even if you are not making money. Do you have passion for your job? Your business? Your dream? Do you love it? If not, be brave and make the necessary changes to find the passion you need to create a fulfilling life. Find a solution, a different path, a new focus.

> *Keeping my focus on having a balanced*
> *life helped me to achieve it.*

Ask yourself, "Am I following my dream? Does my dream match the lifestyle I really want? Am I happy with my life?" You can actually achieve your dreams and lead a fulfilling life, but first you must make sure that the dream you want aligns with your purpose and allows you to align with your needs and the needs of your family. Find out the one thing you are supposed to be doing every second, minute and hour in a day, so that you don't miss a valuable time that you cannot regain.

I know what fear is like. I've been there, and if I could overcome it, so can you. In my work, in my lectures, and in my books I share advice about how to achieve anything you want:

Find focus, success and balance and you have the best chance to achieve your dreams. Whatever dream you have, once you have these essentials, you can achieve anything.

Be you, the unique you. Stay focused.

Get something going.

Stay engaged. Do not be afraid of failure. It may help you to define yourself.

Be confident. Be passionate. Be consistent. Do not procrastinate. Do it now.

I know what fear is like; I've been there,
and if I could overcome it, so can you.

Do not let fear exhaust your energy, or measure yourself by other people's success. Instead, collaborate and network with others to learn more. Practice the process of evaluation and review to determine where you are and where you are going. Discover your productive peak and utilize it to the maximum.

With focus, all is possible. When you are more focused, the tendency is that you will be more productive. You produce more by maximizing your time and you generate more revenue. Your business will also yield more profit for a better lifestyle.

Finally, I always advise people to know their story and to tell it well so that others will learn from it. Now, you have heard my story, the changing moment of my life. Love it, learn from it and lead with it. Let the journey begin.

Florence Onochie is the President of FNO Professional Services Inc. and Vice President of HCO Inc., managing the firm's accounting, tax operations and computer-aided drafting and design department. She has worked in various managerial, teaching and accounting positions, including financial director to the director general of IBC.

Florence has served as member and board member in several professional and humanitarian organizations, including the Rotary club, the Professional Women's advisory board, the National Association of Public Accountants, the National Association of Black Accountants and the National Association of Women Business Owners. She is also an Ambassador of the United States during World Forum, co-founder of the International Women's review board, founder of the Florence Onochie Foundation International and IBC Hall of Fame. Florence is also an inspirational and motivational author.

Florence received numerous awards: gold medal for United States; Board of Governors Award; Woman of the Year in 2000, 2004, 2007 and International Woman of the Year 2010; Ambassador to the World Congress of Arts, Sciences and Communications, 2010; and was featured in Marquis Who's Who among American Women, Who's Who among Americans *and* Who's Who in the World. *She has been featured in* The New York Times, USA Today, Miami Herald, Indianapolis Star *and* Indianapolis Recorder. *She has degrees in accounting, finance and teachers' training. Connect with Florence at www.FlorenceOnochie.com, www.FlorenceAuthorSpeakerCoach. com and www.FNOBooksCalendarsMagazines.com.*

Angela Eleazer

Faith Will Get You Through

Philippians 4:13 *I can do all this through him who gives me strength.*

Shock and fear flooded my heart. *What?* I thought. *They must've gotten it wrong somehow.* But sitting in the exam room, staring at the doctor with a blank look on my face, I couldn't deny it. What had started as some symptoms and a simple scan had turned into something else completely.

There was something on the scan, a spot on my brain. My neurologist, as calmly as he could, in this exam room that smelled like antiseptic, told me—I had a brain tumor.

I had a plan for my life. It was 2005, and I had completed six-and-a-half years of undergraduate and graduate work, earning degrees in electrical engineering, computer science and finally computer science engineering. I'd been president of the Black Engineers Association. I had worked for two outstanding engineering firms, traveling the world for my work, for almost twenty years. I owned my own house before the age of thirty-five. It was a blessed life, and I wanted to continue on to have a family and retire happily. That was my plan. God had a different plan for me.

It had started slow, but it picked up pace over time. I began feeling numbness in my legs and my face. I developed vision problems and excruciating headaches. It continued to get worse—I remember walking from my desk with friends and having to stop for a break halfway to the cafeteria downstairs where we were going for lunch. It was only one flight down! I needed to have these symptoms checked, in case they got even worse and prevented me from even going to work.

I went to my neurologist, whom I'd been seeing for a mild case of multiple sclerosis. He sent me to get some scans, and when the scans were returned, I was met with the news of a spot on my brain—a tumor. And all my expectations fell apart in that moment. As I listened to the doctor talk, I could sense my plans falling through one by one—I could no longer imagine working, filling my home with a family, retiring, living my life. So I sat, dumbfounded, lost, while inside I prayed fervently for another answer, another explanation. *Anything but this.*

There was something on the scan, a spot on my brain.

There was no other explanation. I needed treatment, and fast. Thankfully, my neurologist knew of a surgeon in town who could work with me to remove the tumor. There was nothing else I could do—I set up the appointments I needed and I prepared myself for the risks, for the battle to come.

I was terrified. I hid it, for my parents' sake, but as surgery grew closer, it became harder and harder to hide. I told my friends about what was happening and watched the shock and the pity on their faces. I tried to joke my way through it, to ease the tension. But I was so scared. It was a difficult time, and I hardly knew how I would make it.

My family and my friends carried me through. The day before surgery, my house was filled with them—family, friends, coworkers, classmates, church friends—fifteen people all came to a prayer party for me. We ate, and laughed and expressed our wishes to God for healing and for His presence the next day during my surgery. But after they left, the house felt emptier, bigger. I have never felt so alone as I did standing in my kitchen, the remnants of the party ready to be cleaned up, the walls still lingering with the warmth of all those people who came bearing their love and faith to support me.

And then there it was; there was something I had almost forgotten, and remembering it turned my life around for the

---

God had a different plan for me.

---

better: I claimed to have faith in Christ and an optimism that I was supposed to rely on. That faith and that optimism were what would get me through.

The next morning, I saw a pack of people waiting for me—my friends and family, lead by my mother. God had taken away my loneliness, and I found myself receiving a line of hugs, encouraging me more than I could have hoped for, one by one. And then as a group, we prayed to God for His help and guidance until I finally went in to my appointment, uplifted.

It took two surgeries to get the parts of the tumor out that could safely be removed. My mother didn't tell me at the time (thankfully, because I was scared enough!), but the surgeon had informed her that it was much riskier than I knew. One slip to the left, and I would be blinded. One slip to the right, and I would be paralyzed for the rest of my life. But God guided his hands; he didn't slip, and I came out of surgery successfully.

The fight wasn't over, though. I still had to go through special radiation to remove the remainder of the tumor. In light of this, I grabbed one of my closest friends, and she cut my hair very short. When I looked in the mirror, I had to hold back my tears. The surgeons had lifted up my scalp when they operated, leaving a palm-sized bald spot on my head. Now, my shoulder-length hair gone, my shorter hair blended in with the bald spot. I was sad that such an important piece of me was gone. But thankfully, my hair grew back.

I had six weeks of radiation ahead of me and I had to fly across the country to Boston to get it done. My father came with me, and a friend's brother welcomed me into his church, so soon enough it felt like home, and I made many new friends. Mainly, though, I went to my daily treatment appointments. Strapped down to a round table, I would lie for an hour, the table spinning as radiation permeated my body. I was worried that the radiation would make things worse, rather than make me better. Most of the time someone would come with me, and I was thankful not to have to go through it alone.

It was my priority to work, to achieve success.

On that table, I prayed. I prayed, and prayed and prayed, and I smiled at the nurses and chatted with other patients in the waiting room. Those six weeks seemed like forever, but there was always a prayer in my heart and a smile on my face because I knew something that could get me through.

My mother used to say, "Take a break. Think happy thoughts. Laugh. Sing a song. Tell yourself it's going to work out better than you can even imagine."

And it worked. It did work out better than I could imagine. My life was absolutely changed, and for the rest of my time here on earth; but I believe the change was for the best, and I thank God for getting me through.

The news that the tumor had been successfully treated was so well-received. Remission is a beautiful word, and hearing it come from my neurologist's mouth was a blessing. I could go on with my life—but not as I had before. No, too much had changed, and I was able to recognize my limits and forget my own plans and instead look to God for what I needed to do, rather than what I was supposed to want for myself.

After five years, my neurologist said, "I think you need to stop working now."

If you trust in God when things are going well, He'll see you through when things are not.

I'm not sure what caused him to come to his conclusion, but I was grateful, because we were in a cycle of layoffs at work, and it was a relief to be spared from that anxiety. I'm off work and on long-term disability. Before the tumor, that would've been unthinkable—I was too determined to work, work, work. It was my priority to work, to achieve success. But now, I understand that it is more important to be a blessing to others than to be successful just for myself. I am grateful to have had all my opportunities—to have done the work I have done, to have traveled the world and seen so much of it. But I have new goals now.

The most important thing is to exemplify the love of Christ. I don't live any longer to be graded on my educational and professional performance. I don't spend my days and nights worrying about money and how my bank account will look when I retire. I don't worry about my plans and what life will have in store for me.

If you trust in God when things are going well, He'll see you through when things are not. I've learned to press on, just a little bit longer. God will see me through, and I believe He'll see you through as well.

And here's what you need to do. Trust in God and focus on what's positive. You can't let negativity overwhelm you. I almost did—that night, after the prayer party, I almost let it consume me.

I let myself feel alone and I mourned the future that I thought was being taken away from me. Only by trusting in God and remembering my faith in Him did I make it through the next morning and through the next several years. And He can take you through your painful times, to give you the strength to bear up and keep pressing on. He can bear you up through the bad times, as long as you live in faith and optimism.

Angela Eleazer is a computer science engineer who has worked with Intel Corporation and Hewlett-Packard Company. She established a Poetic Expressions business, customizing personal, religious poems for people, and has worked with various St. Paul Baptist Church ministries, assisting with tutoring and hospitality.

She received her bachelors of science degree from the University of California at Davis, as well as her degree in electrical engineering and computer science. It was here that she served for a time as the president of the Black Engineers Association. She went on to attend The Johns Hopkins University with a fully paid GEM fellowship, earning her master's in science degree in computer science engineering. She went on to work for Intel Corporation, ensuring that the Folsom site computer network ran sufficiently, and then to Hewlett-Packard Company as a technical marketing engineer and a team leader ensuring that support engineers were equipped with the latest knowledge of the company's network management tools.

Now she works from home, writing her stories and spreading her message of living a life that trusts in God, and she works to exemplify the love of Christ.

Teryn Ashley

What Have You Done with Your Gift?

"Ma'am, I am Detective Rodriguez from the Miami-Dade Police, and I am sorry to inform you, but your father is dead."

I blurted, "What?! That can't be true! Not my father."

This had to be some kind of misunderstanding. My father just couldn't be dead. But the detective said, "Ma'am, we found your father dead in his apartment."

Devastated, I fell on the ground and cried. Images flooded my brain: as a child reveling in those rare moments when I got him all to myself and had his full attention or the enormous smile on his face as we colored or played together. And then, after my parents divorced, our Sundays together—Dad's day—when we would go to lunch or to the park, and I got to know him better and connect with him more strongly.

The tears gushed even more fiercely as I relived our last phone call—after Dad moved to Miami, when I was twenty. I had planned to visit him. We had gotten on the phone to firm up all the details and our conversation suddenly became heated. Dad, usually so laid back, said some very hurtful things, and I hung up.

And then, the might-have-beens. Dad never called back to apologize. I never went to Miami. I eventually got married, had a home of my own, started a business, had a baby—and Dad never knew. He never knew any of it and, now, wasn't able to be a part of any of it either. He was dead.

As his only living relative, I had to make all the arrangements. Still in complete shock, and having to keep it all together, as my daughter was six months old at the time, I felt as though the whole world had crashed in on me.

I thought, *How am I going to make it through this? Why is this happening? What am I going to do?*

Then, as though a switch flipped, I knew: *You're going fly down to Miami and take care of this whole mess, and you're going to be just fine. You have friends and family around you who love and support you, and you will make it to the other side.*

And I did. I flew to Miami, got a death certificate, packed as many of his things as I could and shipped them back to my home, had his body cremated and closed out all of his affairs. It wasn't easy, not by a long shot, but I made it, and I did it with the help of others. My support system of family and friends got me through it. That was a huge lesson for me.

"Ma'am, we found your father dead in his apartment."

At the same time as I was getting divorced, my business was growing and my client base was getting bigger. I felt overwhelmed! Then, I reminded myself of what I had just gone through with my father's final arrangements: *If I can make it through that, I can certainly make it through this.*

So, I reached out to my support system and enlarged it by making new business connections. And before I knew it, all the things that I was stressing about—not knowing how to handle the growing pains in my business and fearing it would completely crumble—could be overcome. And they were. Again, I made it!

And, from that moment on, the importance of creating, building and using a network, a support system that one can reach out to, was ingrained in me. A support network is imperative. It can lift you up, bring you out of a slump, create possibilities you've never thought of before, teach you valuable lessons you never knew you needed and, when you have problems or questions, it can help you find answers that you couldn't imagine on your own.

Maybe you're thinking: *I'm sick of this job, sick and tired of working for these people who don't know what they're doing. I desperately want to work for myself, become an entrepreneur, but I don't know where to start.* I would say: "Find someone or a group

---

A support network is imperative.

---

of people who know what they're doing or who are involved in something that resonates with you; seek out groups, or people, who are involved in what you would like to do or what you think you would like to do. Start exploring. You will come across all sorts of people. Maybe you meet Joe Smith today, and although he doesn't have an answer for you, he might lead you to another person who does."

I believe networking is an extremely valuable tool that starts a chain of events. A support system helped me get through crises in my personal life. Networks can help everyone, whether they are dreaming about starting businesses, developing their businesses or charting new horizons. You'll find answers to your questions, encouragement, inspiration and renewed vibrancy. Participate actively in like-minded groups, such as the eWomenNetwork. Don't hesitate to share what you know and what you've learned. Let me share some examples of how networking helped me grow and expand my business. The best relationships are built when both parties add value.

A client that was getting ready for a huge product launch needed me to do twenty-five webinars at the same time. That takes twenty-five computers, because you have to do one webinar per computer. I didn't have all twenty-five computers then, so I was in a panic. Eventually, I told myself, "Let's see who can help me." I reached out to my support system, my network. I called a business friend of mine, who knew a computer guy, who could get me some computers right away. Then the client's copywriter went missing; I reached out to my network and hooked them up with a copywriter. Another close contact put me in touch with someone who could help man the webinars. It was a mad scramble, but, with the help of my support system, everything came together. Without those relationships created through networking and growing my support system, I never would have been able to pull it off.

Networking can bring opportunities beyond what you imagine. I joined a mastermind group, but at first I didn't get involved. When I started participating, going to the meetings, interacting with other people and showing up at the webinars, I

I believe networking is an extremely valuable tool that starts a chain of events.

---

learned a lot of helpful information for running my business: how to become more efficient; how to prioritize and which things that I was handling that I could outsource.

But the big surprise came when I reached out to one of the other members. I wanted to pick this person's brain about certain things I hoped to accomplish. Instead, they picked my brain about another subject altogether and they found what I had to say really valuable. Later on, this person approached me and proposed a partnership of sorts in a different area of business. I don't think there was any chance in the world that I would have met this person outside of the mastermind group. And here we are, building something that is going to be huge!

I encourage you to grow and maintain support networks in your personal and business life. All too often we hide behind our computers and loathe to get out and meet people face to face. Make the effort, please. Human connection is such a powerful thing. Talking with someone about something that you enjoy, or do, or want to do is such a powerful thing! Mere use of our words causes a mental and physical reaction.

When I am having a completely uninspired day and feel like just crawling under the covers in a big ball, if I force myself to follow my schedule, go meet that person I had an appointment

---

Talking with someone about something that you enjoy, or do, or want to do is such a powerful thing!

---

with or go talk to the people that I had planned to get together with, even if I don't want to, I find that, every time, I end up leaving that meeting or that event so happy that I did—and maybe with a new contact, or idea or revised inspiration.

I am so thankful to have my support system. Through it, I have met some pretty wonderful and amazing people, made life-long friendships, solved problems I thought were unsolvable and grown so much as a mother, business woman and friend. With a support system in place, you can handle almost anything—business challenges, impossible dreams and even personal struggles. Reach out. Build your network. Nurture it. Grow it. Believe in it. Call on the people in your network when you need them. They will answer.

Teryn Ashley is an entrepreneur and speaker. She is the founder and CEO of MyAVEditor, a premier multimedia service company, providing online webinars, webcasts and teleconferences for rising stars and rank beginners in a wide range of industries, including Internet marketing, real estate, professional speakers and higher education. With the help of her tight-knit team of technical experts and customer service professionals, Teryn has helped her clients earn millions in launch revenue. As CEO of YourOnline MarketingPro, a reputation marketing firm, Teryn helps her clients create, maintain, enhance and protect their reputations, and then use those reputations to catapult their businesses to success. Connect with Teryn at www. YourOnlineMarketingPro.com.

Beautiful Wild Free: A Beginning

Exhausted after a full day of work, I arrived home late one night, opened the front door and entered the darkness. As I walked into the house, my heels clicked on the floor, greeting me with a very loud, unfamiliar echo. Without turning on the lights, I began to realize what had happened.

After eleven years of marriage, my husband had moved out. The shock of an empty house left me reeling in confusion. I was exhausted with life, exhausted with the familiar feeling of not being good enough, exhausted with begging him to see me... really see me. As though life itself was being drained from my body, I sank to the floor with my sleeping baby girl in my arms.

Physically, emotionally, mentally, I was certain that this would be the one crisis that I could never overcome. Surely, this was the blow that would take me out completely. I cried for hours and I lost track of time. There was no one I could call; there was no one who could understand the extent of this pain. The journey to this point had been traveled imperfectly by my husband and me, alone. We were both responsible for what appeared to be a tragic failure. I had given more than I had to give to a marriage that was never satisfied, to a husband who didn't seem to care if I suffered.

I felt dejected, fooled and crushed with disappointment as I lay on the floor, my body heaving with every cry and breath. But it was on that floor, in a single defining moment, that God met me and gently picked up the shattered pieces of my spirit, shattered beyond my recognition. He met me there, right where I was, and flooded my heart with His love.

Suddenly, I didn't feel as if I was alone. I was accompanied by a great, warm Presence. God reminded me that in my weakness, He was strong. This was not an opportunity to give up on His abilities; instead, this was an opportunity to give up on my abilities. I had to give up on the belief that I had to do it all by myself, that I was alone and that I would never recover. This was my opportunity to let go and allow Him to be God. This was the beginning of my ultimate love-encounter with God.

I began to experience my love-encounter with God, beginning with my own personal meditation practice. This was a time that I dedicated to listening, feeling and recording the knowledge and wisdom that God impressed upon my spirit in a delightful, soothing way. Just as with anything you devote time

---

After eleven years of marriage, my husband had moved out.

---

and energy to, over time, I came into a deep knowledge of what I was studying: God and my Self. As a result, I was restored, more strongly, more radiantly than I can recall with any previous awareness. This delivery of restoration reverberated throughout every aspect of my life, from my spirit and relationships, to my career, business, family and ministry.

During this time, Beautiful Wild Free–Spiritual Healing for Women Rediscovering Themselves, was birthed. Women began contacting me as they experienced the inevitable challenges of life, looking for answers. "Why?" they asked, and, as we engaged in conversation, I discovered that a process of rediscovery was a natural result of having been spiritually broken. It doesn't really matter what did the breaking—the loss of a child, a marriage, a relationship, health—it was simply the fact that there was a breaking that positioned them perfectly to embark upon a journey of restoration that would exceed any understanding of possibility or expectation.

I wrote a parable to assist people on their own journeys of restoration:

THE PARABLE OF BEAUTIFUL

Beautiful runs, escaping through the dense bush, her hair flowing behind her, the breeze kissing her cheeks, the heat of the sun warming her skin. Fresh air fills her chest sharply, like a baby's first breath. These feelings are foreign, new. The pain of bondage can no longer be felt throughout her body. She can still see the marks on her wrists and arms, but the familiar ache that she had learned to live with for so long is gone. In its place is a blank slate, an undefined opportunity.

"This is good," she muses, as in the beginning, even the world was without form, and void. But from that, God created. GOD CREATED!

She keeps running, gratitude for freedom spilling out of her soul in the form of thankful tears. As her forward movement creates momentum, she can hear the echo of her former self calling out faintly, asking her to return to the way of thinking that kept her in bondage. Asking her to return to what was familiar. "Surely freedom is too risky," her past warned. "You don't know what's going to happen—you aren't in control!"

Despite these negative headings, the sweet abundance of her beautiful, wild and free self beckoned her forward, forward into the unknown, forward into trust and forward into the Divine.

After she ran for what seemed like forever, the initial exhilaration of freedom wore off. Beautiful had been running for days, occasionally seeing a wandering tribe here and there. The tribal people were friendly enough, giving her food and water, sharing what they had with her. However, none of them were able to give her directions to where she wanted to go. No matter whom she asked—even if it was the oldest, most traveled member of the group— the most they could do was point her in the general direction.

She was searching for this place of dreams fulfilled, this place where her hopes would be realized, this place of Life Abundant she had heard stories of many times in bondage. From bondage, Beautiful would hold onto the bars of the small castle window, where she could look out and see women passing by in caravans. She would see women who looked as if they had what she had always desired. To her, they looked happy and content. Sometimes, a smile would flicker at her lips when she looked out, and her broken spirit would momentarily grasp the concept of hope while observing freedom. This hope seemed to give her strength.

The others would chide her, believing that looking at what she didn't have would only create pain in that void in her heart over time. "Looking at what you don't have is useless if you can't have it," they would say to her. They had stopped looking long ago.

Most thought this place of Life Abundant was just a tale, but a few of the women in bondage thought that it very well could be a real place. Like Beautiful, they believed that, if they just got a chance, they too could realize the fulfillment of this distant land of freedom and hope.

Beautiful traveled for days, her feet becoming blistered and sore. Her back ached from sleeping among the overgrown roots of trees in the bush. She was surviving, but waves of fear were beginning to wash over her. She was scared.

"I am alone," she told herself.

"At least you had company and a better place to sleep," her past whispered.

"I could just go back," she thought. "It would be easier than this." But in that very moment, her spirit remembered the hope that it had felt in bondage and urged her forward. It couldn't live without exploring the possibilities that it knew existed.

"How do you know this hope is real?" she asked her spirit.

"I've never seen it, so how do you know?" she said out loud to herself as she watched the dusk spreading over the foggy bush.

Her spirit was quiet. "HOW DO YOU KNOW!?" she screamed in anger, out into the darkness, tears streaming down her face, the pain in her chest so powerful she felt as if she was breaking into a million shattered pieces.

Crumbling to the floor of the forest, she wept— she wept for years of feeling lost, feeling inadequate, feeling forgotten, and with every cry, these feelings of lack flowed up out of her. She rocked back and forth, dizzy with the overwhelming lack of what she had always desired and hoped for. The emptying out of her spirit caused her body to feel weak. She could barely move, exhausted from the pressure of release. After what may have been hours, she looked up and realized that she had fallen right by a river.

Gathering slight strength, Beautiful crawled closer to the river, and looked into the soft ripples of water. She faintly viewed her reflection in the water—she hadn't seen herself since she was a child. This was the first time in a very long time, and she blinked with startled recognition. She remembered what she used to look like and was surprised she even recognized herself after all she had been through.

"How do I know? I just know," her spirit softly replied. "I know, because I put the desire for hope in your heart."

Beautiful gasped, not breathing momentarily in the stillness of the moment. She could hear clearly. It was the voice of the Holy Spirit, speaking to her through her own spirit. In an instant knowing, she received that her spirit was right. Even though she hadn't seen her reflection in years, she was still real. She was REAL.

Even though she hadn't seen the things her spirit spoke of, "They are REAL," she realized. They are REAL.

"You can trust me," her spirit said to her. "I am connected to the eternal source of all knowledge, God Himself. If you spend time listening to God speak to you through me, all things will become clear."

Just like this water, Beautiful thought. She slowly eased into the gently flowing water, and let the ripples wash over her, washing away the dust from days of travel, the Spirit washing away the residue of doubt and unbelief in her heart. "Hope," her spirit said to her, "Hope is where it all will begin for you."

What would you do to leave behind the pain and brokenness? What would you do to discover peace, to wake up vibrant, to embody radiance that illuminates that life path you're walking? At the base of all created things is an energy of love. Love has the power to restore, create and enliven. It takes more than just a knowledge of love to accomplish this, it actually takes a love-encounter. An encounter with love brings you to your most authentic self, which is a gateway to true personal freedom.

**Love has the power to restore,
create and enliven.**

As you learn to love God, then to truly love yourself, you can then love others—even those who have purposefully committed severe acts of hurt and hate against your spirit. This is when you find true peace and love and when you learn to position yourself to receive what it is your spirit truly desires: to rejoice in the beauty of love, wildly, freely and with abandon. Come with us to this place, and be Beautiful. Wild. Free.

Erin Shell Anthony, MBA, is a bestselling author, speaker and businesswoman whose life purpose is to help women achieve spiritual healing by coming into an intimate encounter with God's love. She is the creator and spiritual catalyst of her women's ministry, Beautiful, Wild, Free: Spiritual Healing for Women Rediscovering Themselves, which has touched and inspired the lives of women around the world. Erin is a successful entrepreneur who has created brands that deliver one goal: supporting and healing the brokenhearted and celebrating the inherent beauty of the spirit of women. Learn more at www. beautifulwildfree.com, @beautiful.wild.free (Instagram).

Sandra Yancey

Conclusion

On our property in Dallas, I keep a personal garden. For years, every day, I would go out and tend it—pruning the rose bushes, dead-heading the asters, pulling up the weeds that crowded the roots between the tulips and the forget-me-nots. As I worked, I would meditate and come back to center. After just a short time in my garden, I would feel rejuvenated and ready to take on the day.

When my business started to shift and demand more of me and things got crazy, I gave up my garden. I thought, *I don't have time for this anymore. I'll hire a gardener.* Except I forgot that having a garden wasn't just about the beautiful display of sweet-smelling, vibrant flowers. It was about *tending* my garden. The garden helped me remember to stay focused on what was truly important in life, prune away the things that no longer served me well and remove the aspects of my life that were getting in the way of growth.

So often, we give up what nourishes us, what inspires us, what grounds us and feeds our soul in an effort to meet the demands of our businesses.

Recently, we held a PLATINUM event for eWomenNetwork. One of the highlights was my laser coaching. I spent a lot of time paying attention to what women were saying about their challenges and illuminating their blocks to success and fulfillment. It was a powerful event, and it confirmed what I knew in my heart: Women need more than business mastery, they need *life* mastery.

Creating a Life Mastery Retreat for women has been one of my greatest joys. Built on four key pillars—reflection, connection, direction and action—the three-day event is designed to give entrepreneurs a balanced model for success. We take time to reflect on where we've been, to notice the skills and talents we haven't given ourselves credit for and the old resentments we've been holding onto that prevent us from moving forward. Then we build real, meaningful connections to the other attendees—beyond name, rank and business. And we connect to *self*—understanding our limits and our resistances.

With the help of powerful thought leaders, I then offer direction, providing ideas and strategies we all need to think about when growing our businesses. And I do laser coaching, sharing what I see, overall themes, and tips and practices to put

----

When my business started to shift and demand more of me and things got crazy, I gave up my garden.

----

into place to help shift the needle toward massive success. Finally, we get clear on the actions required of individuals in both their business and personal lives to achieve real, lasting fulfillment.

In the process of coming back to myself, in the midst of my own period of doubt, fear and crisis, I reclaimed my garden. I'm in charge of the hyacinths again, the potted ferns and ivy, and the rows and rows of tulips and daffodils. My new Life Mastery class is a way for you to tend your garden for three concentrated days, and then go back to your life with a practice in place that will see you through to the realization of your dreams.

As we close this book, I'm reminded of a story from my first book, *Relationship Networking*. It's called The Daffodil Principle, and you can find it on page 109. It tells the story of a woman who reluctantly agrees to go with her daughter to pick up her daughter's car. As they approach a hill, the woman realizes that they are not going to pick up the car: They come around a bend, she sees a field of daffodils—thousands and thousands of daffodils cascading down the hill.

In the process of coming back to myself,
in the midst of my own period of doubt,
fear and crisis, I reclaimed my garden.

The woman and her daughter talk to the woman who tends the daffodils and learn that she started in 1958 and planted every single bulb by hand—all fifty thousand of them. We included the story in my book to illustrate the point of starting today. For *this* book, I think the last sentences of that story are especially relevant:

"It is so pointless to think of the last hours of yesterday. The way to make learning this lesson a celebration instead of a cause for regret is to only ask, 'How can I put this to use today?'"

How can you use the lessons offered in these stories to move yourself forward? How can you use the powerful messages shared by this book's authors to reclaim your garden?

About Sandra Yancey

Sandra Yancey is an award-winning entrepreneur, international speaker, philanthropist, movie producer, bestselling author and transformational expert who is dedicated to helping women achieve and succeed. She is the Chairman and founder of eWomenNetwork, a complete success system for connecting and promoting women and their businesses worldwide.

Sandra is the author of *Relationship Networking: The Art of Turning Contacts Into Connections,* and is a bestselling co-author of three books, including the first two books in her "Succeeding" series: *Succeeding In Spite of Everything* and *Succeeding Against All Odds,* both number one Amazon bestsellers in multiple categories. With Julie Ziglar Norman, Sandra co-authored *Mastering Moxie: From Contemplating to Creating Absolute Success.* She is also featured in *Chicken Soup for the Entrepreneur's Soul,* which showcases some of the top entrepreneurs in North America.

Big Girls don't cry...
(maybe sometimes, briefly)
...instead, they get
down to business!

Big things happen when you think, act and perform big. You and I both know there are infinite possibilities for you... let me help you:

- Grow your brand
- Monetize your gifts
- Strategize your next steps
- Accomplish your bodacious vision
- Coach you every step of the way

Would you like to work with me?

"It's time to JOLT and get down to business."
Visit: WorkWithSandraYancey.com to get started.

Sandra Yancey
Founder & CEO, eWomenNetwork, international award-winning entrepreneur, bestselling author, movie producer, philanthropist and transformation expert.